SOUGHT

through

PRAYER

and

MEDITATION

SOUGHT

through

PRAYER

and

MEDITATION

A PRACTICAL GUIDE
FOR PEOPLE IN RECOVERY

The Reverend John T. Farrell

Las Vegas

Central Recovery Press (CRP) is committed to publishing exceptional materials addressing addiction treatment, recovery, and behavioral healthcare topics, including original and quality books, audio/visual communications, and web-based new media. Through a diverse selection of titles, we seek to contribute a broad range of unique resources for professionals, recovering individuals and their families, and the general public.

For more information, visit www.centralrecoverypress.com.

Publisher: Central Recovery Press
             3321 N. Buffalo Drive
             Las Vegas, NV 89129

18 17 16 15 14 13   1 2 3 4 5

ISBN: 978-1-937612-33-7 (paper)
      978-1-937612-34-4 (e-book)

Cover and interior design by Marisa Jackson.
Author photo © by Olan Mills. Used with permission. All rights reserved.

To Tom, Jack, and Dan

MY THREE SPONSORS
OVER THE DECADES

I Am Worthy: A Prayer for All Those in Recovery

Rev. John T. Farrell

I am worthy of recovery, serenity, and a happy life. I am worthy of achieving these things, no matter what I have done up to this point in life and whatever transgressions I may have committed. I am still worthy.

I am competent and intelligent, no matter how badly I did in school and what my employment history is. I can make a contribution, no matter what anyone has told me to the contrary. I alone have the means to reach my dreams. I am worthy to live my dreams.

The road of life is difficult, not just for me, but for everyone. It does me no good to compare myself to others. All are worthy in the eyes of God and all face unique challenges. I shall be honest about who I am and will move away from my preoccupation with self. It is not humility to be something I am not or what others expect me to be. I will be myself because I am worthy.

No one will give me my new life of recovery. I am willing to work hard for it. I am willing to accept the gifts and tools I have been given. I am willing to transform myself into the good and worthy person I was meant to be. I am willing to pray and to serve others. I will always remember that I am worthy. And I will always be grateful.

From *Guide Me in My Recovery: Prayers for Times of Joy and Times of Trial* by The Reverend John T. Farrell, PhD. © 2010 Central Recovery Press.

INTRODUCTION

In the world of twelve-step recovery the Eleventh and Twelfth Steps focus on continuing a spiritual life of growth and action for people. They are urged to pray and to meditate. It is assumed that they have experienced a spiritual awakening and have acquired a set of spiritual principles that will guide them in their daily conduct. The dilemma for many people is that while they may have become adept at recovery and living the Twelve Steps, they received little or no guidance in the practical management of their spiritual lives. The purpose of this book is to provide a set of spiritual practices that will appeal to people in recovery as they set out to improve their conscious contact with God *as they understand God* and to practice the principles of recovery in all their affairs.

Much has been written on the subject of meditation and even more on the topic of prayer for people in recovery. Lists of so-called "recovery" spiritual principles are bountiful. But little has been written on the subject of spiritual practices that will assist one's recovery. By spiritual practices, also known as spiritual discipline, I mean the consistent performance of actions and activities undertaken for the purpose of cultivating or developing spiritual growth.

This book provides an introduction to various spiritual disciplines that will assist people not just in "working" the Eleventh and Twelfth Steps, but in helping them develop a set of spiritual practices that they can use in their daily lives and recovery. Although anyone seeking a spiritual life may find this book useful, it is primarily directed toward men and women in twelve-step recovery programs who wish to enhance and deepen their spiritual lives as Step Eleven directs: *We sought through prayer and meditation to improve our conscious contact with God as we understood Him, praying only for knowledge of His will for us and the power to carry that out.*

Spiritual practices are exactly what the name suggests: they are intentional methods to better our understanding about matters of the soul and to assist us on the path to the spiritual growth crucial to long-term recovery. Spiritual practices are tools for becoming aware of the divine spark of goodness dwelling within us all. At their best, these practices stimulate our consciousness with aspirations and visions that transcend the mundane and negative in our lives. In applying spiritual practices, we will find that lines can be blurred between what is considered spiritual and what is material.

Most of us resist the idea of spiritual transformation when we first encounter a program of recovery. I know I did. To live a spiritual life was very different from the life that I had learned and practiced until the moment of my recovery. I was frightened and skeptical. As part of their resistance, most addicts will find all sorts of reasons to divert and distract themselves from the Twelve Steps, especially Step Eleven. But somehow God's will prevails and we overcome our resistance. Our persistence and patience are the means of grace given to us by God, as we strive to create and maintain a conscious contact with our Higher Power.

In finding the path to spiritual transformation, twelve-step programs make clear distinctions between religion and spirituality. Religion is regarded as being laden with theology, doctrine, and worship. Spirituality is perceived as something clearer, purer, and, well, more spiritual. Many of the people I know in recovery describe themselves as "spiritual, but not religious" (for brevity's sakes, I'll use SBNR). And certainly, some of the most faithful, integrated, and compassionate people I know are SBNR.

But the line between religion and spirituality is not always clear-cut. For instance, the common assumption that SBNR individuals operate outside the world of organized religion is not correct. One recent researcher claims that many of the people who regularly or irregularly show up at American churches and synagogues apply the SBNR label to themselves. Scratch below the surface of an average worship service, she says, and you will find many who resonate with this description. They may attend church on Sunday, but during the week pursue meditation, new and alternative spiritualities, wellness programs, and competing claims of ancient wisdom. Oftentimes, clergy themselves are among them. These SBNR people often say their various pursuits are a useful adjunct to traditional religious practices. Conversely, they claim traditional religious practices are a useful adjunct to more contemporary or alternative methods. In fact, it might be more accurate to refer to the SBNR population as seekers, since it seems that their purpose is to connect with that which is greater than themselves—that which is considered divine.

For many in recovery, religion and spirituality can be separated. For me it works a bit differently. I see my religion as something relatively fixed and my spirituality as something dynamic and fluid. Together in me, religion and spirituality act in a creative tension between my spiritual stability and my spiritual growth. I have been an Episcopalian for many years. As such, I am an active member of the American branch of the Anglican Communion. I accept its doctrines and love its worship. I doubt that this will change. At the same time, in the almost forty years of my recovery, I have studied and practiced many different forms of spirituality. Some didn't work for me. Some have been only passing. Some have become permanent. All have helped me grow. In this book I hope to pass along some of the spiritual practices—*not* my brand of religion—that I have learned.

People in recovery ultimately ask themselves the same questions all people do: "Does my life have purpose? What gives my life meaning? When I am most discouraged, what gives me the power to return to the struggle? What are the things that have most decisively shaped my way of seeing and moving into life? Am I worthy of enjoying the fruits of a good life?"

A seminal figure in the psychology of spirituality, James Fowler, suggests that people go through various stages that emerge in regards to meaning in their lives. This starts with the intuitive, imitative faith of childhood through conventional expressions of belief, leading to the development of more independent faith to the universalizing, self-transcending faith of full maturity, as exemplified by spiritual leaders like Bill Wilson, Dorothy Day, Desmond Tutu, Father Mychal Judge, Thomas Merton, Mother Teresa, Rabbi Abraham Herschel, and the Dalai Lama. It is my belief that people engaged in active addiction often leave the path of spiritual growth early in life by rejecting imitative and conventional beliefs, but then fail to replace them with anything positive. They remain angry, resentful, or indifferent toward spiritual growth. But the Eleventh Step forces us to change these attitudes.

One of the lessons absorbed in my own recovery is that using various spiritual practices gives me a heightened sense of connection to God and to the community. It is simply not possible to be an island in recovery. We need others, their company, their love, and their support. We need a Higher Power and its company, love, and support.

The Eleventh Step is very specific. It directs us to pray and meditate in order to maintain a conscious contact with God. Then it remains silent, that is, it leaves the business of how to pray and meditate strictly up to us. This, of course, speaks to the enormous spiritual freedom we are given in our lives, to pick and choose how we grow. It also frightens many of us who don't have any real sense of how to pray and meditate. This book will fill in some of the gaps by discussing the ways in which I have learned how to improve my conscious contact with God as I understand God.

In the course of my recovery I have been deeply influenced by three schools of spirituality: Celtic, Anglican, and Benedictine. The first taught me how close I am to the spiritual world. From the second I learned about my worthiness as a person and about my part in God's creation. The third gave me a sense of stability in my life and in my relations with others. All have affected my recovery positively.

Celtic spirituality offers a way of looking at the world that is earthy and visionary, grounded and transcendent at the same time. It's a form of spirituality that allows me to live fully in the world as a productive member of society while simultaneously understanding the world as a deeply spiritual place fully connected to powers that can enlighten and ennoble me if I seek them and if I allow them.

The Celtic spiritual tradition speaks repeatedly of places that give all people access to the magnificence and wonder of the presence of a Higher Power—not just the holy or the chosen. The Irish call these places "thin places," and the instances when they occur "thin times." According to a Celtic saying, Heaven and Earth are only three feet apart—in thin places that distance is even smaller. A thin place is where the curtain that separates Earth from the spiritual realm is pulled back, and we are able to grasp a world of goodness and beauty beyond our understanding.

Here is a description by contemporary poet, David R. Leigh, of an encounter with God in a thin place:

Every now and then, you find a way—
In your plan—to break through our
   calloused perceptors
And you penetrate our spiritually cataracted sight
So that we find ourselves in seemingly thin places,
Worn areas in the fabric of the cosmic veil,
And there we encounter you.[1]

Thin places invite us to step from one world into another, which can involve entering places that are unfamiliar to us or where we feel less in control. In a thin place the unexpected, the unknown, and the unpredictable become the means of growth. Mountains, hidden caves, lonely moors, seashores, forest glades, streaming water, gardens, churches, monasteries, and deserted paths are often regarded as thin places. But I've come to learn that I can experience God—that is, love, truth, beauty, community, authenticity, honesty, compassion, and connection—just about anywhere and anytime. For instance—and I mention this as a shared experience that will indicate most of us already know something about spiritual practices—one thin place and a thin time for me is a twelve-step meeting. Accordingly, I count regular meeting attendance as a spiritual practice.

Sometimes at a meeting I feel myself connect to everyone who has gone before me in their search for a better way of life. When I am at a meeting, especially during a difficult time in my life, I can feel afraid but not lost. I find a peaceful presence in the company of brother and sister addicts who offer me shelter and guidance. As I sit quietly, just listening instead of dominating, I can hear the words, "Do not be afraid, all will be well, all will be well." Such sentiments can also be found in books, at churches, or in schools, but in a thin place there is a rawness to the experience that transforms words of faith into words of life. In such a sacred place and time, the spiritual and the material planes for a moment become one.

There have been moments at meetings where I become suffused with a sense of joy and connection the likes of which I never knew before. At these times I feel so much at one with the room, with the people, the world, and with God I think that time itself has stopped. My body feels like it is tingling. I imagine that I am glowing. I believe that even breathing is unnecessary because I am so much a part of the cosmos. I have come to recognize these rare occasions as spiritual experiences.

Always upon returning from a thin place I feel cleansed and renewed. I sense an increased awareness and appreciation for all the thin places in my life. From experiencing the divine spirit at a meeting, I can now sense it all around me. I become sensitive to the sacredness of spaces where people of goodwill gather to love and serve. From this vision of connection I have begun to understand the world as an essentially good and friendly place, not as an evil and hostile environment. My fears have diminished and my certainty has diminished equally. I have learned much about living life on life's terms.

The godliness I experience in this one humble place on Earth inspires me to look for other thin places on my journey. Meetings, of course, are not the only thin places in my life. But the great benefit of being aware of eternal space and time is that I can always revisit these divine experiences through my recollection and in my mind's eye. If I ever sense a drought in my worship or contemplations, all I have to do is imagine I'm on my way to my home group and filling my heart with the power of recovery. I hear the voices of recovery and sense the holy cadence of divine love.

Whether I am physically present at a thin place or have returned to one in my imagination, I experience God's presence and receive the peace of this Celtic blessing.

Deep peace of the running wave
Deep peace of the flowing air
Deep peace of the quiet earth
Deep peace of the shining stars
Deep peace of the Son of Peace.

A second spiritual influence for me has been Anglican spirituality, the vision of life underpinning my religious life. Anglicanism embodies the spiritual vision of the Church of England and is rooted in the Celtic spirit. Its traditions encompass a two-thousand-year history that begins with the Celts, the original inhabitants of the British Isles. These people were first Druids, then Christians, who brought their Earth-based attitudes to bear in their new religion. While Anglicanism has sustained many other influences and developed its own style, it has never lost the Celtic sense that holiness and spiritual understanding are accessible and available to all.

Anglicanism is "incarnational," that is, it believes that God has entered fully into human life and history. This belief engenders a "down-to-earth" spirituality that affirms the goodness of life and the created world. In short, Anglicans believe that the extraordinary is found in the ordinary and the divine is everywhere. It also teaches that everything God creates is good because God is Infinite Good and cannot make or be anything that is not good. This elevated view of the human condition was best expressed by St. Athanasius who wrote, "God became human that humans might become God."[2]

The so-called Anglican ethos has guided my life in many ways. Through understanding its optimistic and hopeful vision of humanity, I have become more open-minded and accepting, since Anglicans believe that truth can be found in exploring the creative tension between opposites. For example, I have learned to affirm the sacred and the secular, the material and the spiritual, the mind and the heart, glory and intimacy.

When I was in my active addiction I could be intolerant, intransigent in my opinions, and "black and white" in my thinking. Now I have learned to affirm the ambiguity of personal experience and the breadth of human life. I search for wisdom in many places and encourage people to listen to each other and bring their honest questions to their life journey. I am much more at home in the world of poetry, imagery, symbols, storytelling, rituals, and art. I believe that beauty, in all its fullness, is a doorway to truth, goodness, and God.

Anglicans avoid extremes, believing that a godly life is one that is both inwardly graceful and ordered, and outwardly serving and responsible. Perhaps through our

Celtic origins, Anglicans have a reverence for nature and its rhythms. We are not above the created order, but very much a part of its delicate and intricate balance.

By embracing the Anglican ethos I have been able to flesh out the Twelve Steps and gain shape and focus for my vision of what a recovering life of integrity, dignity, and connection with others would look like. To put it briefly and bluntly: I am a hell of a lot easier to get along with and a much nicer guy!

A good portion of my increased good temperament and ability to get along with people is due to acquiring a sense of stability and balance in my life. It will seem odd to many that some of the best guidelines for achieving balance and stability in our world, where anger, stress, and angst have become the norm, come from a sixth century Italian monk, who at one point chose to live by himself in a cave. Yet through the centuries, millions have found the teachings of St. Benedict of Nursia and his rules for monastic life key to their own spiritual wholeness. I am an extrovert and an occasionally intrepid world traveler, so I have no intention of becoming a monk. But Benedict's teachings on prayer, work, community, and fellowship have become the guiding principles of my heart. I try to carry them wherever I go so that my life will remain balanced and stable.

The spirituality of Benedict, also called Benedict-inism or the Benedictine ethos, has offered those who follow its path a way to faith-filled living through work, prayer, learning, and living in community. This is not a spirituality that requires a departure from everyday life, but rather a way of being that embraces and becomes fully engaged in the goodness that permeates our daily existence. It offers us a real structure in which "to practice these principles in all our affairs."

For me, sustaining a decent and ordered life of any kind was hard enough in a world that I viewed as hostile and that had me going around in circles—from the stresses of my profession to the demands of my personal life to the rigors of complete abstinence to acquiring a new way of life and back again. Getting a spiritual life seemed like a luxury to be put off to another, quieter time. Learning more about the Benedictine way, however, led me to believe that the search for a spiritual life begins not in some exotic, unreachable place, but right where I am, in the midst of all the craziness. It starts within my busy, stressed-out human heart, not in some other "more spiritual" place. The more I am able, therefore, to be my true self, the more successful I would become in developing a spirituality that would be real and satisfying.

The solid, common sense advice on how to get a spiritual life, no matter how busy your day, is embodied in Benedict's insistence that his monks follow a Rule of Life. A Rule of Life is an intentional pattern of spiritual disciplines that provide structure and direction for spiritual growth. He believed that a rule establishes a rhythm for life that reflects a love for God, a desire to connect in love with others, to follow a moral structure, and to respect the creation around us. The disciplines that we build into our rhythm of life help us shed the "old self" and allow our "new self" to be formed. Benedict, of course, wrote a rule that is still followed today. I will discuss this aspect of Benedictinism in more detail in a later chapter, as well as how to write your own Rule of Life as a spiritual practice. At one point in my recovery I wrote a rule exclusively for myself to follow. I combined it with a creed (a statement of what I personally believe) and, with many edits, still try to follow it today.

Writing a rule changed the way I think about myself, how I treat others, and how I spend my time. I was able to ask myself to identify what is really important in my life—what outweighs all my desires for money, status, and success, and what points to the authentic spiritual self deep within. I was finally able to overcome the difficulty of nurturing my spiritual health in a world where the sacred is seen as something separate from everyday living.

When I live an integrated life, I can express the true identity that was created for me, as it is created for each of us. My every encounter and activity revolves around my longing to be connected. Benedict's wisdom can help us all center ourselves even while we live day in and day out in a culture that may work against us. Moreover, it shows us how those who share our lives are part of the spiritual way.

Prayer, of course, is the ultimate spiritual practice, followed quickly by meditation. Let me therefore conclude by offering a prayer that may be of help as you begin reading this book as part of your own spiritual journey:

> *God, as I understand you,*
> *I pray to keep my connection with you*
> *open and clear from the confusion*
> *of my cluttered mind and untidy daily life.*
> *Through my prayers and meditations*
> *I ask especially for freedom from the bondage of self.*
> *May I overcome my lapses into intransigence,*
> *self-justification, grandiosity, self-pity,*
> *depression, anger, and wishful thinking.*
> *Grant me the guidance*
> *of gracious thought and graceful action.*
> *May your will, not mine, be done.*

Prayer of Acceptance

REV. JOHN T. FARRELL

Source of my strength, never allow me to become victim to self-pity and despair. Help me realize that life's futility begins and ends in waves of piteous self-indulgence. Help me avoid self-pity and despair. Let me accept life on life's terms, not mine. Amen

From *Guide Me in My Recovery: Prayers for Times of Joy and Times of Trial* by The Reverend John T. Farrell, PhD. © 2010 Central Recovery Press.

A NOTE ON TERMINOLOGY

In its earliest days, twelve-step meetings were Christian in their outlook. The founders of Alcoholics Anonymous (AA) were members of the Oxford Group, a nondenominational, evangelical, and Protestant organization. Before the book *Alcoholics Anonymous* was written, the early AA members used parts of the Bible and Christian devotional literature to aid them in their recovery. For these pioneers, the use of the term *God* presented no difficulties either theologically or intellectually.

This quickly changed. In the late 1930s and early 1940s, some people seeking recovery were skeptical and leery of an approach to spiritual growth that was so Christocentric and Bible-focused. When the Twelve Steps were written down and the Big Book published, the members were given an option. The Second Step referred not to *God*, but to a "power greater than oneself," and the Third Step qualified *God* by adding "as we understand Him." Today, as a result of this freedom, members of twelve-step groups tread innumerable paths in their quest for spiritual growth.

When they first enter recovery, people in twelve-step programs are encouraged to use anything they wish for their God or Higher Power. Stories abound of people using things like a bedpan, a table, a doorknob, a stone, a Barbie doll, a mountain, a sports car, or "Good Orderly Direction" for their Higher Power. In theory, you can pray to your sponsor, a statue, or your home group itself as your God if you wish.

Most people, of course, are more interested in developing spiritual lives based on something more meaningful than regarding God as a bedpan. It is to those people that this book is directed. Throughout I will use the terms *God* and *Higher Power* as synonyms. We are all seekers. We all want to believe in something. We all arrive at our own conclusions. With that in mind, I use *God* and *Higher Power* as shorthands for whatever complex or simple concepts lie behind the terms for each individual reader.

For instance, some people believe in a theistic, personal God who is an entity separate from humanity and who acts as Creator, Redeemer, and Sustainer. For others, this understanding of God can no longer be affirmed with integrity. For them another sense of God may be possible, that is, understanding God as pure spirit, essence or as mystery or truth. For still others, a Higher Power is an intellectual construct, consisting of a set of principles or values or virtues that guide life and behavior. Ultimately, I think as recovering persons we want to believe that we are not merely subservient to a Supreme Power, but that we are part of a Ground of Being that is greater, more powerful, more wonderful, and more beautiful than we are individually. And it is one of our greatest longings to connect to whatever *it* may be.

CHAPTER ONE

What Are Prayer and Meditation?

There are as many ways of praying as there are people who pray, a diversity that is surely encouraged in the world of recovery. By the time we reach Step Eleven we have become abstinent, accepted a Higher Power in our lives, taken inventory, forgiven ourselves for our misdeeds, and made amends to others. We have truly accepted a new way of life and seen the transformation of ourselves into productive members of society. We enjoy life and take pride in what we have accomplished. At times, we are even happy, finally grasping that our happiness comes from within, not from without. Now is the moment to consolidate our gains by forming the basis of a truly spiritual life by *improving our conscious contact with God.* According to the Eleventh Step, we do this through prayer and meditation.

What are prayer and meditation? The most succinct definitions I have ever encountered are that prayer is talking to God and meditation is listening to God. I also like the definition from the 1979 *Book of*

Common Prayer that says, "Prayer is responding to God, by thought and by deeds, with or without words."[3] I focus especially on the term "responding" because it integrates the act of listening as well and therefore suggests that meditation is a part of, or the end result of, heartfelt two-way communication. For me, meditation has always involved trying to hear the "small, still voice" inside me that the prophet Elijah so eloquently described.

Prayer, of course, has many purposes. For those who think "improving conscious contact" is a little vague, you might consider some other options. Prayer, for instance, can be a way to seek God's guidance, to express gratitude, to become closer to the divine, to help others, and to improve our lives.

In this chapter I will describe the seven types of prayer, while Chapter Two will offer suggestions for ten methods of prayer and meditation that might be helpful to a person in recovery. I will also recommend books and web resources that will allow you to further study any method you may find appealing.

The principle types of prayer can be divided into seven classic categories: adoration, praise, thanksgiving, penitence, oblation, intercession, and petition.

Adoration and **Praise** are the lifting up of our hearts and minds to the God of our understanding, asking nothing but to enjoy God's presence. God is certainly worthy of our praise and adoration. Many of the most beloved prayers are psalms written in praise of God.

King David surely knew this when he sang, "Blessed are You, Lord God of Israel, our Father, forever and ever. Yours, O Lord, is the greatness, The power and the glory, The victory and the majesty; For all that is in heaven and in earth is Yours; Yours is the kingdom, O Lord, And You are exalted as head over all."[4]

Thanksgiving is offered to God for all the blessings of this life, for our recovery, and for whatever makes us better persons and draws us closer to God. In recovery terms, this is about having an attitude of gratitude. There is a short prayer of thanksgiving that I use every morning: "For each new morning with its light, For rest and shelter of the night, For health and food, For love and friends, For everything Thy goodness sends."

Penitence is about taking moral inventory, sharing our misdeeds, making restitution, amendment of life, and asking for forgiveness. In the days of the Oxford Group, the process of penitence was simply called "coming clean" and is now incorporated into Steps Four through Ten. When I wish to ask God's forgiveness, I often use a prayer first brought to my attention by Stan Meyer, which, like all good Jewish prayers, does not mince words:

> *For the sin which I have committed in*
> *Your sight through arrogance of my will,*
> *And for the sin which I have committed*
> *before You by breach of trust.*
> *For the sin which I have committed in*

Your sight by casting off responsibility,
And for the sin which I have committed
before You by denying and lying.
For the sin which I have committed in
Your sight by evil thoughts,
For all of these, O God of forgiveness,
forgive us, pardon us, grant us atonement. Amen.[5]

Oblation is an unusual word that means "offering." It harks back to ancient times when humans made sacrifices to the gods. Today, prayers of oblation are offerings of ourselves, our lives and labors, in service to the divine. To me, one doesn't *recite* a prayer of oblation; one *lives* a prayer of oblation. I try to make my life a prayer to the God who brought me to recovery and who guides my life toward goodness and service.

Intercession and **Petition** are flip sides of the same prayer coin. The first brings before God the needs of others; in the second, we present our own needs that God's will be done.

Prayers of intercession are essentially prayers of generosity. Here we forego our own concerns and focus on the needs and wants of others. We feel sorrow over the pain, loss, grief, or sickness of our friends and families and we ask God to relieve those travails. We hear of natural disasters and we pray for the victims. We abhor war and we pray for peace. We pray for the success of others. We pray that others will "make it" in the program. We pray because we connect with others and because we have foregone some of the self-absorption that was so much a part of our active addiction. We learn that by praying for our enemies, we can love them a little more and understand them a little better. The lesson here is that through recovery we have learned to connect both with God and others. Prayers of intercession complete the circle of connectivity with the divine and with humanity. This is how we express our understanding that no one is an island.

Prayers of petition can be spiritual pitfalls if they come from a place of selfishness or pure self-interest. God is not interested in fulfilling our selfish needs. Nor is God interested in hearing our foxhole prayers—that is, prayers where we attempt to strike a bargain with God. As in, "God, if you get me out of this jam, I'll go to church or I'll be nicer to my wife or I'll even go to a meeting."

In fact, most spiritual masters agree that prayer is not about asking, it is about connecting. So, as tempting as it may be to ask God to fix my problems, find me a relationship, get me a job, smite my enemies, obliterate my failures, ensure my success, and even arrange for my recovery, I have learned my relationship with God doesn't quite work that way. Instead, I have learned to ask God for grace to grow in my character so I can achieve positive results in my life. I also pray to accept things in my life or in the world or people in my life, all of which are beyond my ability to change. It's not merely a cliché when we tell newcomers that the only thing we can really change is ourselves.

This understanding of petition is especially helpful when it comes to prayers of healing. I'd like to use myself as an example here. I suffer from a variety of chronic medical conditions, some serious (coronary artery disease, congestive heart failure, a low ejection fraction), some potentially dangerous (sleep apnea, clinical depression), some just annoying and damn painful (gout, plantar fasciitis). In the last four years my life has been circumscribed by my conditions.

None of these things are curable, but all are treatable. I have trained myself not to pray for cures nor for a return to life before my first heart attack nor for relief from pain. Instead, I pray for acceptance. I pray for strength. I pray for my caregivers. I pray for the discipline to follow directions in terms of medications, physical therapy, diet, and exercise. I pray that I continue to find ways to be useful and to make a contribution. I pray that I do not become isolated and disconnected. I pray for gratitude, for my friends, for good healthcare for myself and for all people, and for the gift of life I have been given. While I understand that my life must be lived in the context of my medical issues, I pray, and will always pray, that my life will never be overwhelmed by them.

CHAPTER TWO

Types of Prayer and Meditation

As my spiritual development unfolded in recovery, I learned that my initial perceptions of how to pray were limited. I grew up thinking that there were only two ways to pray: either in quick, silent words or at worship in church where most of the praying was done by ordained clergy wearing silken vestments unique to their order. It was also made clear the latter form of prayer was the superior. In fact, the church had basically outsourced prayer to a professional class.

It wasn't until after I became one of those silken robe-wearing, ordained professionals myself that I began to understand what a disservice the church had done in allowing people to think that a priest's prayer, any priest's prayer, was more favorable to God's ears than their own. Yet another way to describe prayer and meditation is finding our way to walk with God. Every one of us has a different walk and, while there is only one journey, we all follow different paths. It may be the priest's task to set you on the path, sometimes even to lead you on the path, but the path is yours alone and the walk is yours alone.

Here are a number of different methods that I think may help you on that path:

Praying with Music

Over the years I have learned both to pray in my own way and to pray with others. I've also learned a lot about the practice of meditation. One thing that has helped me immensely in my meditative practices is music. It has been said that there is nothing in the world so much like prayer as music. This comment has guided me in my recovery as I seek through prayer and meditation to improve my conscious contact with God.

From the very beginning, music was for me a natural means of experiencing communion with God and with the world around me. In the ancient world, philosophers believed in *musica universalis* (literally "universal music" or "music of the spheres"), a philosophical concept that regarded the proportions in the movements of celestial bodies as a form of music. To hear the music of the spheres was to experience perfect harmony and to connect with God.

Nature is based in musical sounds if we consider the music of birds singing, of seaside waves crashing, of bees buzzing, of crickets chirping, of ice crystals crackling, and of raindrops splashing. Often musical composers and performance artists attempt to replicate some of these patterns of nature in their own music. When that happens, my soul is able to resonate with this music and feel a closeness to perfect love, which is God.

What kind of music works for me? In recovery, I've focused on softer, gentler musical forms to meditate authentically and to hear the small, still voice in which the God of my understanding speaks. Here are some types that I find helpful:

- **Classical music**: "Why waste money on psychotherapy when you can listen to Bach's B Minor Mass?" asks composer Michael Torke. Good point! Classical music is a wide field, of course, but I've found eighteenth-century and Renaissance music to be best for meditation. Gregorian chant is wonderful as well. All of these are low-key, mellow, and rely on repeated rhythmic patterns that are conducive to meditation.
- **Fusion**: Fusion is a type of music that utilizes repetitive structures to incorporate musical techniques from the classical tradition, jazz, and the contemporary pop world. Michael Torke, quoted above, composes music in this style. Claude Bolling was an early fusion composer. A group called Il Divo is probably the best-known band of fusion singers.
- **New Age** or **Ambient**: New Age is broadly defined as relaxing, even "meditative" music that is primarily

instrumental. Similar to New Age are Celtic music and smooth jazz. There are many, many artists in these forms. As I write this I'm listening to Steve Halpern. Enya is an absolute favorite. There's a label called Wyndham Hill that lists most of the major composers and artists.

Why wait? Light a candle, close your eyes, breathe deeply, and flow with the music.

Praying a Daily Inventory

> *"In the morning form your intention*
> *and at night examine your conduct."*
>
> —THOMAS À KEMPIS

For me, the inventory suggested in the Tenth Step is the practice of looking into my heart to discern the motivation for the things I do. When I make it part of my prayer routine, it becomes part of the Eleventh Step as well. Each day I ask myself questions about what I plan to do and about those things I have already done. These questions focus on how I can use my ordinary life to show love and service. In this practice, I try to evaluate my activities based on how well I love, rather than other standards. This helps me be aware of opportunities to love and serve, and also prompts me to connect with my Higher Power for the strength I need to offer others the love I receive from God.

Ideally, I try to divide my inventory into three parts during my day: In the morning, I get out my daily planner and look at my day. I ask myself:

- What activities will give me an opportunity to show love for God?
- What activities will give me an opportunity to show love for others?
- Then I envision "three rings" (Love of God, Love of Recovery, Love of World) and fit the activities for the day into the appropriate circle. I ask myself:
- What situations will I face today where it will be easy to show love and be of service?
- Where will it be difficult to show love and be of service?

It helps when I pause in the middle of my day to reflect about how things are going. Around noon, I ask myself these questions:

- What happened since this morning?
- Who have I come in contact with?
- Have I shown love for all and treated all with respect?
- What is occupying my thoughts today?
- How am I being of service to others today?
- Where am I being called to be specifically this day?

- Is it time to make a tough decision that I have been avoiding?
- How have I shown gratitude for the blessings in my life, especially my recovery?

And in the evening, I ask myself the following:

- Have I been a good memory in someone's life today?
- When did I find it difficult to love others?
- Were there times that I lost sight of my purpose?
- Looking over my day, what motivated me? Love of God, love of recovery, or love of the world?
- Did I work with joy?
- Did I wait with grace?
- Did I help, or at least connect with, another addict today?
- What do I know, but live as though I do not know?
- What needs my attention?
- Will tomorrow be a better day?

Listening as Prayer

So goes the old proverb:

A wise old owl sat on an oak.
The more he saw the less he spoke.
The less he spoke the more he heard.
Why aren't we like that wise old bird?

In my active addiction I never listened to others. To begin with, I was too busy talking. And while I may have heard what others said, I never listened to what was behind their words: the needs, the dreams, the yearnings, or the fears. In recovery, however, that has changed. As I've learned to love and connect with others, I've become more like that wise old owl and I learned to listen. Listening has become an important path in my walk with God.

Listening is a lot easier than I imagined. Time is on my side. Thoughts move about four times as fast as speech. With practice, while I am listening I have learned I am able to think about what I am hearing, really understand it, and give an appropriate and caring response to the speaker.

In my morning meditation I try to focus on my upcoming day and make a resolution to do something positive. Today, for example, I resolved to spend some time on two essential skills of the recovering life: listening and speaking. I'm working at home this morning and have several important phone calls to make. I shall seek to apply the gift of my listening skills to these interactions. In the afternoon, I have to go out to meet and speak with others, including saying a few words at a public event in the late afternoon. As I meet with people, I shall seek to share thoughts that demonstrate mature and responsible responses to their concerns. I shall try to connect with others always. Then in the evening, I shall spend some quiet time praying for all whom I have listened to throughout the day.

Praying the Hours

The custom of reciting prayers at certain hours of the day or night goes back to Judaism and is an integral part of prayer in Christianity and Islam. The Psalms are rife with pronouncements on the value of praying at specific times of the day: "I will meditate on thee in the morning" (63:6); "I rose at midnight to give praise to thee" (119:62); "Evening and morning, and at noon I will speak and declare: and he shall hear my voice" (55:17); "Seven times a day I have given praise to thee" (119:164). Early Christians observed the Jewish custom of praying at midnight, terce (9:00 A.M.), sext (noon), and none (3:00 P.M.)—naming the prayers themselves after the hours of the day). Later, Islam applied a regimen of rigorously observed prayer at certain times of the day.

At their beginning, the Christian versions consisted of almost the same elements as the Jewish: recital or chanting of psalms followed by a reading of the Old Testament. To this was soon added readings from the Gospels, Acts, and Epistles, and later collects, intercessions, the Apostle's Creed, and canticles. Eventually these cycles of prayers became known under different names: the Daily Office, the Divine Office, and the Liturgy of the Hours. By the time St. Benedict wrote his Rule for Monasteries, the Daily Office included prayers at seven distinct times of the day: vigils (several nocturnes throughout the night), lauds (sunrise), terce (9:00 A.M.), sext (noon), none (3:00 P.M.), vespers (sunset), and compline (after sunset, before bed). In the sixteenth-century, the *Book of Common Prayer* reduced the Daily Office to four: matins, noonday prayer, evensong, and compline. In the Roman Catholic Church the practice of the Divine Office is honored in the requirement that priests recite a daily breviary (a book containing a specific selection of liturgical rites).

Praying the Hours is not for everyone (unless, of course, you're a monk or nun). I've only honored the practice at times in my life, although I promised my bishop at my ordination that I'd do it according to the *Book of Common Prayer* daily. But I understand that the Hours represent deep images of the rhythm and movement of the day and that to pray the Hours (in whatever version, and there are many) is to be in harmony with the sacredness of the day and the meanings of light and darkness. And when I've had the discipline to do this, I've been the better for it.

If you're interested, I recommend four resources. The first, and best, is a book called *Seven Sacred Pauses: Living Mindfully Through the Hours of the Day* by Macrina Wiederkehr. The author updates the Divine Office in refreshing ways and makes it seem both desirable and possible to pray the Hours in the classic fashion of seven times a day. A special CD, *Seven Sacred Pauses: Singing Mindfully Dawn Through Dusk*, has been created by Velma Frye as a companion to the book.

The traditional minded can use the *Book of Common Prayer*, which includes a two-year lectionary of Biblical readings. Another traditional resource is Phyllis Tickle's *The Divine Hours* in several volumes. There are several online versions, the best being that offered by the Universalis website at universalis.com.

Centering Prayer

Centering prayer—also known as contemplative prayer, *apophatic* prayer (related to the idea that God can only be understood in terms of what He is not), or mantra meditation—is a method of silent prayer that prepares us to receive the gift of prayer in which we experience God's presence within us, closer than breathing, closer than thinking, closer than consciousness itself. This method of prayer is both a relationship with God and a discipline used to foster that relationship. Centering prayer is wordless, imageless, and contemplative. It is emptying oneself to be filled with the presence of God.

Centering prayer is an age-old form of connecting with God, but has been popularized in our time by Father Thomas Keating, a Cistercian monk. He promotes it as a way to add depth of meaning to all prayer and to facilitate the movement from the more active modes of prayer—verbal, mental, or emotional prayer—into a receptive prayer of resting in God. Centering prayer emphasizes prayer as a personal relationship with God and as a movement beyond conversation to communion with the divine.

Here are the guidelines for a beginning method for centering prayer:

- **Choose a sacred word.** This can be any word that expresses your intention to be in God's presence. You can ask the Holy Spirit in a brief prayer for inspiration as to which word might be especially suitable to you at this time. Some examples of sacred words are: Amen, Love, Trust, Yes, Peace, Faith, Silence, Calm, and Stillness.
- **Sit comfortably.** Be comfortable enough so that you are not distracted by any thoughts of discomfort, but not so comfortable as to encourage sleep. You can sit on the floor, on a cushion, or in a chair. The important thing is to balance your body in an upright position, so you feel relaxed yet alert.
- **Time: Twenty minutes.** Aim to spend at least twenty minutes and up to thirty minutes in centering prayer. If twenty are too much at first, you can do a shorter session rather than not doing it at all. But twenty or more minutes is ideal because something starts to happen around ten to fifteen minutes that should not be missed.

- **Silently introduce the sacred word.** Once you are settled, silently introduce your sacred word inwardly, gently, as a way of signaling your welcoming of God's presence within. You may have your eyes open or closed, whichever works best for you. Silently saying the sacred word to yourself at the start of the sitting period is a way of reminding yourself of your intention to allow God's presence to fill your space and for God's actions to work through you.

- **Do not resist or react to thought.** When you become aware that you are engaging with your thoughts, or any sensations and emotions that may come up, simply return ever-so-gently to the sacred word. Do not attempt to make your mind blank or to achieve a certain feeling or "state." Resist the urge to analyze your experience or to reach for some specific achievement. Thoughts are a normal part of centering prayer. Simply bring your mind back to the sacred word and rest in its stillness.

- **At the end, remain in silence for a couple of minutes.** This will allow you to readjust to the outside world again and to reconnect with your senses, while bringing a part of the stillness back into the world and into your daily life.

Art as Prayer

Just as some people find prayer through writing, others find art to be helpful. And by art I mean drawing, painting, sculpture, molding, carving, gardening, or creating anything that is visual and tactile. The act of creating images and patterns allows us to break out of normal habits of discernment and as a result fresh and exciting insights emerge.

Many prayerful artists see themselves as collaborating with creation. When they pray they feel they are uniting with a "mysterious Other" in their art making. Sometimes this means noticing resistance to making changes or surrendering attention to their desires and letting go of their ideas. This kind of mindfulness calls for responsive willingness, as opposed to willfulness, betrayal, or refusal to trust—attributes similar to the humility highly valued by those in recovery. Prayerful artists, then, are ultimately seeking moments of vision and movement toward completeness. Part of the process involves the courage to confront obstacles to growth and freedom for the sake of the emerging image. Humility is necessary to allow this image to come into being. It is an acknowledgment that the artist serves a divine intention, not dictated by human will. Percy Bysshe Shelley was speaking of poets, but he might as well have been referring to artists, when he said that they are "almost divine."

Further ideas on this subject can be found in Barbara Ganim and Susan Fox's book, *Visual Journaling*. I am also indebted to Ingrid Slatten, my fellow member of the Order of Urban Missioners, who is currently completing her master's degree in this subject at Fordham University.

Circle Making

According to Pastor Mark Batterson, "Drawing prayer circles around our dreams isn't just a mechanism whereby we can accomplish great things for God. It can be a mechanism whereby God accomplishes great things in us."[6] Like many in recovery, have you ever sensed that there's far more to prayer and to God's vision for your life than what you're currently experiencing? To answer this need, Batterson adapts the legend of Honi the Circle Maker who once drew a circle in the sand and would not budge from inside it until God listened to his prayers.

Circle making encourages us to connect with God so as to unleash our dreams and desires through the efficacy of bold prayer. By enveloping ourselves in a circle of prayer, we are able to identify our heart's longings and desires. When this happens, we are praying the kind of prayer that God delights to answer.

Batterson uses timeless knowledge and tales that predate Jesus to urge the reader to simply drop to his knees. Beginning with the Jewish legend of Honi, who drew a circle around himself and prayed for rain, Batterson examines the answered prayers of several "circle makers." The circle metaphor is applied loosely throughout the book (for example, walking in prayer circles, praying in a group, praying repeatedly for a concern), making it accessible in multiple situations. Readers who like this approach will appreciate his intensity and encouragement to pray "tenaciously." The unearthed technique may have you drawing prayer circles around everything from buildings and articles in the news to your own hopes and dreams.

Batterson has written two books to explain his method, *The Circle Maker* and *Draw the Circle*. There's also a workbook, *The Circle Maker Prayer Journal* for those who may want to use this as another method of journaling.

Franciscan Prayer and Meditation

Many forms of spirituality and consequently many approaches to prayer have developed in the Western tradition, but the three greatest, or at least most popular, have been those associated with Francis of Assisi, Ignatius of Loyola, and Benedict of Nursia. Each of these is associated with a particular spirituality and a particular approach to prayer. By "particular," I mean a specific system, or schema of beliefs, virtues, ideals, and principles that form a particular way to approach God and therefore all of life in general. These approaches are not contradictory, but simply represent the idea that there are many paths on one journey.

Let's start with Francis, someone who resonates deeply with those in recovery. While most spiritual masters have left voluminous writings and teachings to guide us, Francis has mostly left us the example of his own life. After all, he was the one who, when speaking of God as love, advised us to preach love, using words only if necessary. Francis spoke to us through the deeds of his life rather than through his writings, and his wholehearted, enthusiastic practicality is a challenge to us today as we search for meaning and fulfillment in our way toward God. Cornerstones of the Franciscan approach are humility, fraternity, and penance (if that doesn't sound like a program of recovery, I don't know what does!).

Francis had an incarnational approach—that is, he saw God in relational terms. God was his Parent. God was his Brother. God was his Sister. God was the Spirit of Love that lived within him. Francis did not speak about spirituality so much as he lived his prayers. One of his early followers said, "He became prayer." For Francis, prayer was holding back nothing of yourself for yourself, so that the Higher Power who gives himself totally to you may receive you totally.

We all know the so-called "Prayer of St. Francis" ("Lord, make me an instrument . . ."), so let me end with another, lesser-known example of Franciscan prayer. I love it because it speaks to the interconnectedness of God, creation, and all humanity.

CANTICLE OF BROTHER SUN AND SISTER MOON OF ST. FRANCIS OF ASSISI[7]

Most High, all-powerful, all-good Lord,

All praise is Yours, all glory,

all honor and all blessings.

To you alone, Most High, do they belong,

and no mortal lips are worthy to

pronounce Your Name.

Praised be You my Lord with all Your creatures,

especially Sir Brother Sun,

Who is the day through whom You give us light.

And he is beautiful and radiant

with great splendor,

Of You Most High, he bears the likeness.

Praised be You, my Lord, through

Sister Moon and the stars,

In the heavens you have made them bright,

precious and fair.

Praised be You, my Lord, through

Brothers Wind and Air,

And fair and stormy, all weather's moods,

by which You cherish all that You have made.

Praised be You my Lord through Sister Water,

So useful, humble, precious and pure.

Praised be You my Lord through Brother Fire,
through whom You light the night
and he is beautiful and playful
and robust and strong.

Praised be You my Lord through our Sister,
Mother Earth
who sustains and governs us,
producing varied fruits with
colored flowers and herbs.
Praise be You my Lord through
those who grant pardon
for love of You and bear sickness and trial.

Blessed are those who endure in peace,
By You Most High, they will be crowned.

Praised be You, my Lord through Sister Death,
from whom no-one living can escape.
Woe to those who die in mortal sin!
Blessed are they She finds doing Your Will.

No second death can do them harm.
Praise and bless my Lord and
give Him thanks,
And serve Him with great humility.

Ignatian Discernment

One of the most perplexing issues for developing a spiritual life in recovery is the question of discernment—that is, how do we know what God is asking us in any given situation? We first encounter this question in Step Three and it recurs throughout our spiritual growth. I've come to realize that the challenge for me is that I can never be absolutely certain what God's will is. After all, God is mystery and, by definition, there will always be things unknown and things unclear. The good news, however, is that there are lots of God-given directions that are relatively easy to discern in my life. For instance, I try to live my life according to three principles: that God wants me to continue in my recovery, that God wants me to grow in virtue, and that God wants me to lead a life of service.

Discernment is not just simple decision-making. It operates along the lines of the "spiritual experiences of an educational variety" of which Bill Wilson liked to speak. Discernment is more of a process of learning through experience. We see this kind of transformation all the time in recovery. People come to us in distress with twisted lives and values. Over a period of time, through abstinence, the steps, spiritual growth, and service, they learn a new way of life and become different people, or, as I like to put it, the people whom God meant them to be. They have finally discerned who they are.

Discernment is really about listening or hearing with the heart or catching the music of the spirit. One problem in listening, of course, is knowing which voice is the authentic voice. Which voice is really speaking in your best interests? In the sixteenth century, Ignatius of Loyola, founder of the Jesuit Order, proposed that discerning God's will was a matter of mind, body, and spirit. He developed an "examen" to use that would lead spiritual seekers to hear when God is speaking. He saw the result of the examen as a movement of your heart called your "consolation." By contrast, if something was not right for you spiritually, he called it your "desolation."

In order to seek God's desire for us in a given, concrete life situation, Ignatius advanced the following plan of meditation:

- Go to a quiet place and center yourself. Relax, breathe, and pray for humility and guidance.
- Articulate your question. Zero in on the decision to be made and formulate the issue in a rational way. Be as specific as possible. Write it out, if that helps.
- Open yourself to God's will, and pray for freedom from any unhealthy motives, attachments, prejudgments, or addictions. Pray to be free enough to consider only this value: which choice will express your most authentic self, and give most glory to God?
- Imagine you have already made the choice you are most leaning toward, and try to see what you

would feel like having made it. Do the same [...] the alternative choice(s). Pray continuously for openness to divine guidance, until you eventually focus on one of the alternatives.

- Ask yourself if you are feeling consolation or desolation about your choice. Consolation is a feeling of joy, trust, hope, enthusiasm, love, confidence, and courage. Desolation is a sense of unease, fear, isolation, pessimism, suspicion, anxiety, and lack of energy. If you are experiencing fluctuations between consolation and desolation, you may be under the influence of unconscious motives or unhealthy attachments. If so, continue to ask for freedom and keep opening yourself to God.

- Trust in God and make your decision, even if you are not certain about it.

- Confirm and test the decision. Live with your choice for a while and see whether your thoughts and feelings continue to support it. If not, you may need new information, which you should gather, and then start the process over again.

An important thing to remember about the Ignatian examen is that it need not be something done alone. Read Chapter Four on mentors and see if you'd like a sponsor or a soul friend to walk with you in your discernment process.

Benedictine Stability

Before I found recovery I was a restless soul stalking the Earth to and fro. Discontent, restless, peripatetic, always searching, never satisfied, forever looking to see if the grass was greener over the rainbow, looking for an easy place where my troubles would melt like lemon drops. I lacked steadiness and knew it. But I could never settle down. I always had to move on. I never could stick with anybody or anything. I had no idea, of course, that my *dis-ease* was part of the disease of addiction. It was only when I entered recovery that I learned that I could, over time, achieve the peace and serenity that I so desperately longed for. But first I had to find something else, and that was stability.

Early on I was delighted to find there was a method of spirituality that emphasized stability in one's life. That was Benedictine spirituality—perhaps the most ancient of Western types. Ironically, I had studied at a Benedictine college in my youth and had not paid much attention to the spiritual activities surrounding me. But I must have caught some of it by osmosis because when the time came, I was ready to hear what was being said to me.

Benedictine monks and nuns all take a remarkably countercultural vow when they join the monastery. It is called the vow of stability. They promise to live the rest of their lives in community, prayer, and harmony in the same monastery with the same group of people. They make a life-long commitment to one particular group

of people and one particular place. In many ways, their emphasis on stability is the opposite of the spirituality of St. Francis, who saw the world as his neighborhood and all creatures as his brothers and sisters. Benedict doesn't deny Francis' view. He merely suggests that a spiritual life can be lived in quieter rhythms and harmonies without ever leaving one's doorstep.

Of course, the Benedictine vow of stability is not for everyone and certainly not for me. But it had much to teach me about recovery. First, it taught me to connect with people particularly, not generally, as I had done in the past. Hence, I stopped being the life of the party, the center of attention, and made close friends in the program. I also got a sponsor as a guide and mentor, so I would no longer be facing life alone. Second, it taught me to connect to something greater than myself where I could be *a part of*, not *apart from*. For me, that would be the twelve-step fellowship where I found and continue to enjoy recovery. Similarly, the Episcopal Church also became a stabilizing force in my spiritual life as time went on. Finally, the Benedictine approach taught me about commitment to a particular group of people, with whom I'd stand through thick and thin. For me that became my beloved home group, Angels with Dirty Faces, at 6:30 P.M. every Saturday night in the Upper East Side of Manhattan.

It was through understanding the concept of stability as promoted by Benedict that was I able to understand the deep value of twelve-step recovery, not just as a community but as a community of grace. In its transformation of addicts' lives, twelve-step fellowships act as secular communities of grace, places of spiritual reconciliation and healing, much like Benedict envisioned. Our particular communities, which focus on the stability of recovering lives, allow our members to flourish, to connect with a larger community, to achieve reconciliation for our fragmented lives, and to find healing for our broken hearts and spirits.

CHAPTER THREE

Journaling

Since the invention of writing, people have found ways to express their innermost thoughts and feelings on everything from paper to cave walls, from tablets and papyrus to parchment, and whatever other kinds of canvases were at hand. Long before there were psychiatrists, psychologists, analysts, encounter groups, gestalt therapy, aromatherapy, Zen, and the myriad other approaches to personal growth, spiritual enlightenment, and transformation, people who wanted to search for meaning and perspective in their lives would write their thoughts, feelings, visions, and dreams in a journal.

From Michelangelo to Anne Frank, journal-keeping has historically been a vehicle for releasing tensions, resolving conflicts, working through crises, and connecting with the intuitive inner self—the "person within the person"—that wonderful source of common sense, wisdom, and spiritual guidance that lives somewhere inside all of us, and that becomes far more present and active in our recovery.

In line with this great human tradition, today we keep diaries, write letters, pen poetry, author memoirs, scratch graffiti, create blogs, and fictionalize our lives and experiences. These activities feed our need to clarify and focus experience, to share our lives, to remember, and to record for posterity. Often what we write is for our eyes only and we prefer to keep what we've written private. On the other hand, many of us publish our writings. But the common denominators are that these writings are personal, subjective, and cathartic.

In the last few decades we have begun to better understand writing—or, as it is called in this context, *journaling*—as a spiritual practice. It was only after I started journaling seriously about ten years ago that I was able to uncover underlying long-term patterns in my life. Through writing I was able to track the sense of movement or motion in my life to help me move forward on track. I've been able to look at periods and significant events and see the patterns and see how I've been transformed and how I've grown. Consequently, I can discern ways in which to carry the threads of these movements forward. Journaling has been an invaluable tool, especially when I've been in transition and looking for direction to move into the next phase of my personal and spiritual growth.

A man named Ira Progoff perfected the modern understanding of journaling as a spiritual tool. The former director of Dialog House, Dr. Progoff worked toward a dynamic, humanistic psychology as a private therapist, lecturer, and group leader. He served as Bollingen Fellow and as Director of the Institute for Research in Depth Psychology at Drew University. He was a leading authority on Carl Jung, depth psychology, and transpersonal psychology as well as journal writing. Indirectly, he contributed much to programs of recovery and should be recognized for this.

Dr. Progoff was an expert on the psychology of Carl Jung, who was in turn the psychiatrist who so influenced Bill Wilson. Progoff's thesis, published in 1953, was titled, "Jung's Psychology and Its Social Meaning." He is best known for his development of the Intensive Journal Program and the Process Meditation method. I was first introduced to Progoff through his masterful reworking of a spiritual classic called *The Cloud of Unknowing*.

The Cloud of Unknowing is a fourteenth century spiritual classic that addresses the human need to connect with our creator. The book espouses a specialized type of prayer and meditation on the divine that is designed to allow a person to grow in their knowledge of God. *Cloud of Unknowing* documents techniques used by the medieval monastic community to build and maintain that contemplative knowledge of God. Written as a primer for the young monastic, the work is instructional, but does not have an austere didactic tone. Progoff captures its loving tone and encourages readers to embrace its maternal call to grow closer to God through meditation and prayer.

Ira Progoff believed in the creative potential of all people and was a psychologist of hope. He was exceedingly tough-minded in the sense in which William James used the phrase, that is, unsentimental, matter-of-fact, and down-to-earth. He regarded these habits of mind as prerequisites for journaling. He proceeded upon the belief that when an individual undertakes to bring his life into relation to God, he is embarking upon a serious and demanding task, a task that leaves no leeway for self-deception or illusion. It requires the most rigorous dedication and self-knowledge. Journaling, for him, was about strong and earnest thinking. It makes a realistic appraisal of the problems and weaknesses of individual human beings, for it regards man's imperfections as the raw material to be worked with in carrying out the discipline of spiritual development. In program terms, Progoff would be a great, but tough sponsor.

For some, journaling has been one of the greatest and most freeing experiences in their lives, mainly because by writing they could actually slow themselves down, and think about what was truly happening around them as well as their part in it. Many people in recovery treat journaling as something they "know they should do" but rarely take up the practice of, and if they do, they fall off the wagon within a few months. But it doesn't have to be that way, especially when you learn about the amazing benefits of journaling.

Here are ten ways in which journaling can change your life, or at least significantly deepen your understanding of Step Eleven:

1. **Understanding How We Feel.** Journaling can lead to a deeper and more realistic view of what feelings we are actually experiencing. What addict hasn't experienced what it's like not to know what to feel, or not knowing how they were actually feeling at a given time?

2. **Perspective.** Journaling can give us a better understanding of our own point of view, as well as of what others may think of a situation. It can help us understand the spiritual and ethical dimensions of our life situations.

3. **Joy in Life.** Journaling helps us realize that life is joyful and that our lives are much deeper and more interesting than we tend to be aware of. Through our journals we can better understand how to live our lives to the fullest.

4. **Self-Knowledge.** With journaling we uncover aspirations and ambitions that we never imagined. It can enhance our self-expression.

5. **Posterity.** The idea of writing for ourselves and then being able to pass that writing onto others,

whether it be old friends, children, or grandchildren is inspiring.

6. **Achieve Balance.** Journaling lets us process feelings. Rather than leaving feelings completely bottled up inside, we can put them down on paper and get them out of our hearts and minds so we can process and attain serenity and acceptance.

7. **Storytelling.** Journaling teaches us how to write stories, thereby soothing troubled memories, stimulating our growth, and bringing us to forgiveness of self and others.

8. **Intuition and Creativity.** Journaling awakens our inner voice and enhances our trust in ourselves. It provides insights and improves sensitivity.

9. **Stress Reduction.** Journaling can reduce the scatter in our lives. By bridging our inner thinking with outer events, we find that we are able to detach and let go of the past more easily. We can experience the past through our eyes as a mature adult, not as a troubled addict.

10. **Truth.** Journaling can help us find the truth by encouraging us to be honest. In many ways, our journal may become our intimate, accepting, trusting, caring, honest, and perfect friend.

Here are some suggested methods to incorporate journaling into your recovery:

Step Work

The form of journaling best known to people in recovery, of course, is writing the steps. In the late 1930s, the progenitors of twelve-step recovery worked the steps swiftly and systematically in relatively short periods of time. Stories of Dr. Bob Smith abound of how he would drive newcomers around Akron so they could make amends to those they had harmed and tick off names quickly on their Ninth Step lists. As an extreme example of this approach, Clarence Snyder, AA #3 and founder of that program in Cleveland, devised a method whereby he maintained the steps could be worked thoroughly in one day under his tutelage. Well into the 1970s people would trek to Clarence's retirement home in Florida to intensively work through the steps and come home "recovered." Folks who favor these early methods argue that the only mention of "writing" in the Twelve Steps comes in Steps Four and Nine. We write our inventories and make our lists. And for many, that's it. That's the way it was it written, we might even say.

It was in the 1980s that I first heard of the steps being written under the guidance of a sponsor. It was a novel, even radical idea, and like many novel, radical ideas, it is thought to have originated in California. I am not a cultural historian, but I am convinced that these ideas were imported into twelve-step recovery by people who had taken one of Dr. Ira Progoff's journaling workshops. Progoff was a Jungian psychologist who knew that addiction could only be treated as a spiritual malaise. In the 1970s especially, people were flocking to Progoff's workshops, particularly in California where they were very popular. Some of those participants must have been people seeking recovery who readily adapted the journaling concept to writing the steps. It must have been a natural process for them to make the link. Understanding the benefits, they spread the good news.

Writing the steps is now an accepted method of step work, not practiced by everyone, but widespread in some areas and in some programs. The practice is especially prevalent in Narcotics Anonymous (NA).

The key to writing the steps is a good sponsor (see Chapter Four). A sponsor is a guide through the steps and the one who provides you with direction and focus for your writing. There are a number of excellent workbooks for writing the steps and many sponsors suggest using them. For instance, Dr. Patricia Beckstead has written the *12 Step Journal: One Day at a Time* and NA World Services produces an outstanding book, *The Narcotics Anonymous Step Working Guides*. Others follow the sets of directions they were given when they themselves wrote the steps. Some try to tailor a sponsee's writing to his or her own needs and capabilities.

I am one of the latter types. For instance, I just finished working the First Step with a young man whom I'll call Dexter. Dexter lacked discipline and focus. Part of his addiction was prevarication and passive-aggressive behavior. So I gave him a set of readings from program literature to complete over a month-long period. During that same time, I asked him to call certain older members of his home group to discuss particular topics, like commitment, service, complete abstinence, order, direction, selflessness, sharing, and the like. Finally, I asked him to write three short journal entries defining addiction, powerlessness, and unmanageability. Afterward, we discussed his thoughts on what he had heard and what he had written. Then I asked him to write another journal entry, this time writing why he thought he was an addict and what he wanted to do about it. Through this process Dexter was able to detach himself in some measure from the self-absorption and delusionary thinking endemic to addiction and to look at addiction and the unmanageability of his life with honesty, open-mindedness, and willingness.

Letters to God

Journaling can be an amazing part of how you connect to God. By keeping a record of how God moves in your life, over time you will see how intimately God is involved. Then one day, you will read with awe the testimony God has written on the pages of your life.

One way to make this connection is to write letters to God as a form of prayer. I first encountered this idea in Alice Walker's masterful novel, *The Color Purple*. The story opens with the main character, Celie, and her memory of her father's order to stay quiet about his abuse of her. The rest of the novel is composed of letters, many of them private letters that Celie writes to God. In her first letter, Celie asks for guidance because she does not understand what is happening to her. Only fourteen, Celie is already pregnant with her second child—the result of rape and incest. Walker uses the novel's epistolary (letter-writing) form to emphasize the power of communication. Celie writes letters to God and gains strength, maturity, and compassion from her letter writing.

I have encountered several people in my program world who are inveterate letter writers to God. One of them, Lynne V, has told me that her writing allows her to be focused, to be authentic, and to feel closer to the source of all being. The concept of writing letters to God has been popularized by a film of the same name that tells the true story of Tyler Doughtie, a boy dying from cancer who sustains his faith and life by writing "Letters to God."

Blogging

Blogging is not for everyone in recovery. For some, its public nature puts them off, especially those for whom anonymity is a social or professional issue. Others view anonymity as a spiritual principle that leads them to regard blogging as a way of fostering attention on something that should be private. But for many, maintaining a blog is a good way of instilling the discipline of journaling. By capturing our thoughts, views, and ideas on life, recovery, growth, and spirituality, we are creating a digital record of our goals, frustrations, barriers, and aspirations to share with others. A blog is a way of immortalizing our experiences, strengths, and hopes and to share them with a wider circle.

Another advantage of blogs is that they allow us to contribute to the body of knowledge and wisdom about recovery and the human endeavor that is freely available for anyone to tap into. A blogger can feel immense satisfaction from empowering others in recovery by providing useful information and bits of knowledge that they can use in their own recoveries.

Writing a blog also allows us to have a conversation with ourselves and to embrace an attitude of reflection toward our growth as human beings. We can ask ourselves tough questions, ponder and chew over them for a few days, and revisit the questions again at the appropriate time. For matters that are less sensitive, we can even "poll" our network of readers, fans, and friends online, seeking their views on a decision that is difficult for us to make using our own resources. Their comments and interactions help make the subject matter come alive.

Keeping an online journal further helps us to extend our creative capacity, tapping into our right brains and compelling us to write in a relatively unbridled fashion. Maintaining a blog helps us to quiet our hearts and minds, acting as a conduit through which to expend our nervous energy. In times of difficulties and trials, blogs can act like a constant companion where frustrations, sadness, or fears can be poured out. In summary, blogging can keep us sane in this crazy world, where change is the only constant. It can act as an anchor for our innermost thoughts and emotional life.

Poetry

A little over ten years ago I read a short book that opened up a new dimension of journaling for me. It was a book by a British writer on spirituality, Esther de Waal, called *Lost in Wonder*. The book addresses spiritual seekers who want to slow down, see the world, and regard themselves afresh. To that end, de Waal discusses ideas and methods of seeing with our inner eyes—things like silence, attention, change, dark and light, mystery, and gift are each discussed in separate chapters. De Waal's premise is that people misunderstand the basis of the spiritual life as something that will tell them to "Do this!" or "Don't do that." It isn't. It's "Look!" and "Wonder!" She wants us to learn to give attention to the world around us.

De Waal observes that the African people have a word, *mzungu*, that they use to describe Westerners whom they see as always being restless, unable to sit still, running around in circles, and moving from one thing to another. Instead, de Waal would have us learn the arts of silence and "long-looking."

One of her methods of "long-looking" captured my attention and imagination. She suggested that readers observe the world more closely and appreciatively by writing a poem every day. Specifically, she recommended a poetical form that was unknown to me: a Japanese structure called *tanka*. Since adopting her idea, I have written hundreds of these short poems. Sometimes one every day; at other times many of them in large clumps. Together, they constitute a record of the longings of my heart and my spiritual progress since 2000.

"Tanka" means "short song" and is a traditional form of lyric poetry that has been composed in Japan for over 1,300 years. Tanka is an unrhymed verse form of thirty-one syllables. In English, it follows a pattern of 5–7–5–7–7 and is written in five lines. Tanka has been adopted by many writers in English who have developed their own cultural and stylistic innovations to the form. For instance, I often rely on alliteration to provide "music" to my poems and rarely use capitals, except when referring to God. I also illustrate my tanka, which I think makes the experience of devising them deeper and more significant.

I write my tanka usually as part of my daily meditation routine. My compositions are often sporadic, except in Lent and Advent when I write them daily. Many of my tanka concern God and my spiritual life. I also write about my observations of life, my joys, and things I've seen and experienced. My pets are occasional topics. I love writing about beauty, although I also mark my failures and some of the world's ugliness. When I'm angry, I am capable of writing a "for my eyes only" version I call *tanka of bitterness*.

Here is a sample of several tankas I've written, selected to give you an idea of what they look like and of how personal they can be, not at all "literary" or contrived.

First, a spiritual tanka:
> how should we pray, Lord . . .
> alone, with others, by rote,
> spontaneously, at work,
> at church, at meetings, in the car?
> why not all of the above?

Here's one on recovery:
> from self-absorption
> to selflessness. that is the
> journey we must take
> via sharing, sponsorship,
> the steps, our spirit, service.

And let me end with something more whimsical. I wrote this one on a trip to South America:
> buenos aires,
> the first, foremost big apple.
> boulevards, tango, flashing
> white teeth, great food, shades of
> evita, juan, and madonna.

CHAPTER FOUR

The Spiritual Practice of Mentoring

My junior year in high school was difficult. I was in my active addiction although no one in my family or school had noticed it. I was performing erratically in school. I got in trouble for a variety of adolescent misadventures. The end result was that I was not invited to return to my exclusive prep school, a school that I had enjoyed.

Instead, I transferred to another boys' school that was less socially and academically prestigious than the one I had attended. It was not a good match. I was a misfit from the very beginning, ignored by most of the other students and occasionally ridiculed. I didn't fit in. I was miserable and lonely. I hated going to school every day.

The only bright spot in that horrible year was one of my teachers. The Roman Catholic Church ran the school and many of the teachers belonged to a teaching order called the Marist Brothers.

One of them, Brother Cyprian Rowe, took me by the hand, listened to my troubles, and encouraged me intellectually and spiritually. He made my life bearable and I am forever grateful to him.

But Brother Cyprian didn't just make me feel better. He inspired me with his passion for social justice. He himself was a young man at the start of his own remarkable career as an educator and warrior for justice. He went on to receive his doctorate and became a scholar and a professor at several universities. Cyprian became known nationwide for his outspoken writings and speeches about the place of African Americans in the Roman Catholic Church and the paucity of black leaders in the church hierarchy. Throughout his life, Cyprian Rowe challenged the church to practice the universal principles it teaches, maintaining that blacks had heard the promise but had never seen it delivered.

Brother Cyprian Rowe was my first mentor— that is, an individual in my life who offered me encouragement, shared his experiences and knowledge, inspired me to be greater than I thought I was, guided me when I lost my way, and sometimes just listened when I needed to talk. As a mentor, Brother Cyprian made a lasting difference in my life.

Brother Cyprian was not my last mentor. There was also Dr. George Herndl, my favorite professor in college who taught me to believe in my intellectual gifts and in my ability to write and analyze. Later on there was Father Allan Hohlt, who encouraged me toward the Episcopal priesthood and helped me understand my vocation and my own worthiness. Along that path there was also Father John Midwood, who taught me how to be an effective pastor. And then there were the three men who have been my twelve-step sponsors, all of whom enhanced my recovery in various ways and made me a better person. It has been a particular joy and privilege to work with my current sponsor who was a high school friend and who has known me longer than anyone. I would be remiss if I didn't list my own natural father, with whom I formed a close and loving relationship in adulthood. He was a source of invaluable guidance, and a person I could be certain would always love me no matter what.

I have also had a trio of mentors whom I've never met, but who have inspired me by the heroic virtue of their lives. These mentors, my spiritual guides *in absentia*, have impacted my life deeply by their example and by their words. The first is Father Mychal F. Judge, OFM (1933–2001)—a Franciscan priest who dedicated his life to serving the homeless, recovering addicts, people with AIDS, and as chaplain to the NYC Fire Department. On Sept. 11, 2001, Father Mychal rushed to the scene of the World Trade Center attacks. After administering last rites to a firefighter, he was hit by debris and killed.

At his funeral, Father Michael Duffy said this of Father Mychal: "Mychal Judge loved to bless people, and I mean physically. Even if they didn't ask. A little old lady would come up to him and he'd talk to her, you know, as if she were the only person on the face of the earth. Then, he'd say, 'Let me give you a blessing.' He'd put his big thick Irish hands and pressed her head till the poor woman would be crushed, and he'd look up to heaven and ask God to bless her, give her health, and give her peace . . . ."[8]

Father Mychal had twenty-three years sober in Alcoholics Anonymous when he died in 2001. He was chaplain to Dignity, the organization for gay Roman Catholics, and guided many gay men out of self-hatred and bitterness. His life and ministry will forever be an inspiration for me as a brother in recovery and in the priesthood. I wish I had met him and received one of those fabulous blessings.

Father Mychal left few writings behind but friends have gathered some sayings of his that I use as prayers. Here are just three:

On recovery he said, "Every morning I get out of bed, kneel down, and ask God to help me get through the day without a drink."[9] He would end his days with "Thank you, Lord. Please help me to stay sober, to stay loving You and serving You."[10]

On the need to be honest with self and others: "Thou shalt not bullshit."[11]

In his last sermon, he prophetically proclaimed: "You do what God has called you to do. You get on that rig; you go out and do the job. No matter how big the call, no matter how small, you have no idea of what God is calling you to do, but God needs you. He needs me. He needs all of us. God needs us to keep supporting each other, to be kind to each other, to love each other."[12]

My second source of inspiration is Dorothy Day (1897–1980), who was a founder of the Catholic Worker Movement, which combined radical social reform with her deep faith in a movement for social justice and peace. Initially an Episcopalian, she converted to Roman Catholicism and was inspired by an itinerant French philosopher, mystic, and farmer named Peter Maurin. Taking seriously the command to be responsible for our neighbor, Dorothy Day became a relentless advocate. Her boss was the individual on the street who was forgotten by society; the one we see each day, the one on the park bench who smells of alcohol and urine, the one with the needle in his arm. Over the course of her long life, Dorothy was a beacon to both the poorest of the poor, and to those who were spiritually impoverished. Day set up Houses of Hospitality to help feed, clothe, and comfort the poor. She lived throughout her life according to the Beatitudes.

At her funeral, which was held at Nativity Church in New York, so many people gathered that many ended up having to stand outside on the sidewalks. When she was alive Dorothy did not want to be called a saint.

As Eileen Egan later recalled, Dorothy would often say "Don't call me a saint. I don't want to be dismissed so easily."[13] But since her passing, the word has been used openly by many of her admirers. Dorothy's leadership initiated a "permanent revolution" that was rooted in the Sermon on the Mount for which she had "prayed, spoken, written, fasted, protested, suffered humiliation, and gone to prison."[14]

Dorothy was a prolific writer. She had been trained as a journalist and published her own newspaper, the *Catholic Worker*, for many years. She also wrote books and a spiritual autobiography called *The Long Loneliness*. For anyone interested, I would recommend an anthology published after her death, *By Little and by Little: The Selected Writings of Dorothy Day* (1983). I'm not sure if she had recovering newcomers in mind, but my favorite quote from Dorothy Day is, "They cannot see that we must lay one brick at a time, take one step at a time."

My third mentor at a distance is still alive. I even met him once. He is Desmond Tutu, the Anglican Archbishop of South Africa. Desmond Mpilo Tutu rose to worldwide fame during the 1980s as an opponent of apartheid. He is a Nobel laureate and has traveled the world for the cause of peace and reconciliation. He began his campaign against the apartheid system in South Africa in 1978 when he became the first black general secretary of the South African Council of Churches. In the mid-1990s, he served as chair of the

Truth and Reconciliation Commission, investigating human rights violations under the administration of President Nelson Mandela, and in 1996 retired as the Archbishop of Cape Town.

In 2005 I was the Episcopal Chaplain at Fordham University, New York's flagship Jesuit institution. There was a special convocation to award Archbishop Tutu an honorary degree. The University Church was packed. After the ceremony and service of Vespers, I pushed myself through the crowd to the Archbishop. Not wasting words, I knelt before him and asked for his blessing. I felt electrified to be in the presence of genuine holiness.

I believe God is good enough to give to each generation one or two figures whose commitment to justice, peace, and love is lived out luminously, concretely, and courageously. These figures help us see that living in hope and faith—even in the face of the fiercest opposition—is both possible and necessary if healing and peace are to come to our world. Archbishop Tutu inspires me because I aspire to the values that lie at the heart of his mission and identity.

One of the greatest lessons taught to me by Archbishop Tutu is the value of laughter in easing tension, displacing anger, and connecting with an opponent. There is a story of how he ascended the Cape Town cathedral pulpit one Sunday to preach, yet again, against the evils of apartheid. As he did so, government-dispatched soldiers with machine guns encircled the nave. It was clear that if the bishop dared to speak against government policy, there would be a violent assault on him by the soldiers. When the bishop surveyed the scene from the pulpit, he paused, and then he laughed. Slowly members of the congregation laughed with him. And finally, the soldiers also began to laugh. All laughed together, I suppose, at the absurdity of the scene. When the laughter subsided, Tutu preached against the evils of apartheid. And the soldiers, along with the congregation, listened respectfully.

Desmond Tutu's words can have a special resonance for those in recovery. I was especially moved when he once said, "A person is a person because he recognizes others as persons." When my self-esteem is at a low point I like to remind myself of another remark he made: "We may be surprised at the people we find in heaven. God has a soft spot for sinners. His standards are quite low."

I have other mentors as well: Father Dan Egan, the self-styled "junkie priest"; Danny Carlson, the founder of Narcotics Anonymous in New York; Bill Wilson, the founder of Alcoholics Anonymous; and Esther de Waal, the writer on spirituality I mentioned earlier. These people—along with all of my mentors, alive or dead, known or unknown to me personally—have one thing in common: they taught me how to grow, how to believe in myself, and how to take risks. My life would be vastly different if they had not taken me by the hand and agreed to be my guide. They have all added to my spiritual life.

In finding them and learning to listen to them, we have both engaged in the spiritual practice of *mentoring*.

The word "mentor" itself has a lovely history. In Greek mythology, Mentor was the friend of Odysseus and tutor of Telemachus. On several occasions in the *Odyssey*, the goddess Athena assumes Mentor's form to give advice to Telemachus or Odysseus. Because of Mentor's relationship with Telemachus, and the disguised Athena's encouragement and practical plans for dealing with personal dilemmas, the personal name *Mentor* has been adopted in English as a term denoting someone who imparts wisdom to, and shares knowledge with, a less experienced colleague. His name has become proverbial for a faithful and wise advisor. The first recorded modern usage of the term can be traced back to a 1699 book entitled *Les Aventures de Télémaque*, by the French writer Francois Fénelon. The book's lead character is Mentor. And so it was that the term "mentor," going back via Latin to a Greek name, became the noun meaning "wise counselor." It was first recorded in the English language in 1750.

Today, of course, the process of mentoring is well-known and valued, and consequently there are many terms for our mentors. We can call them coaches, advisors, spiritual directors, tutors, big brothers, rabbis, guides, gurus, or surrogate parents. There are also groups that organize mentoring programs like MENTOR: The National Mentoring Partnership, Mentoring USA, the Maybach Foundation, and the Mentor Network. January is National Mentoring Month. *Mentor* is a journal for professional academic advisers. There's even a TV show called *The Mentor*, featuring top CEOs mentoring small business owners across America.

Mentoring in the secular world focuses on helping young people get a firm grounding in life or in assisting a younger colleague in professional advancement and knowledge. In the spiritual world, mentoring refers to the provision of spiritual direction and is defined as an interpersonal relationship with a spiritual companion in which we learn how to grow, live, and love in the spiritual life. The purpose of spiritual direction is discernment— that is, understanding what God or our Higher Power is doing and saying. It is important that a spiritual director be someone who has a sense of being "established" in God. Otherwise, it can be dangerous to allow an ill-equipped or broken person into our soul space. The best spiritual directors are "wounded healers," people who have transformed their brokenness into a deep spirituality of their own.

In twelve-step programs we call our mentors and spiritual directors our "sponsors." As we all know, nothing compares to the healing value of one person helping another. Every twelve-step program I know recommends that a new member get a sponsor: an older member who will help another member of the fellowship by sharing his or her experience, strength, and hope in recovery and serving as a guide through the Twelve Steps. I recommend getting a sponsor who has more time in recovery than you, and a working knowledge of the Twelve Steps. Any member is free to choose any other member as a sponsor, as long as both parties are in agreement. A sponsor is a guide to help you understand and work your program, including, and especially, the Twelve Steps.

Following are some guidelines and considerations to keep in mind with regards to sponsorship.

1. **Finding a sponsor.** Look for someone who seems willing to build a special, supportive, one-on-one relationship with you. Treat it like an interview and ask yourself: Are we a match? Compare your mutual expectations and see if you are comfortable with each other.

2. **Trusting your sponsor.** Be sure that you feel you can trust your sponsor and that you are safe in the relationship. For many, a sponsor of the same sex will make this more likely. Be aware that he or she will not necessarily become your friend. A sponsor should be loving and compassionate, but also detached and objective enough so as to act as your trusted ally against your own self-deception.

3. **Early on in your recovery.** Your sponsor will introduce you and act as a practical guide to your

program and its culture in your area. This includes your program language, meeting formats, service structure, and the meaning of program principles.

4. **What to expect from your sponsor.** You should know and accept that a sponsor's help is not unconditional. He or she will be with you and support you for as long as they believe that you are trying to grow in your recovery. He or she cannot grow for you, or evaluate your goals for you, or tell you what is best for you. Your sponsor is not a legal advisor, parent, marriage counselor, therapist, or social worker, but simply another person in recovery willing to share his or her journey through the Twelve Steps.

5. **What your sponsor expects from you.** That you be honest and listen with an open mind. That you stay in regular contact, through phone calls and by meeting up in person. Ideally a sponsor will want to form a deep and caring friendship with you, but they cannot stay close to you if you choose not to grow. If your sponsor loses faith in you or begins to feel pity for you, then staying in the relationship will inhibit your as well as his or her growth.

6. **Do not worry about being a burden to your sponsor.** A sponsor benefits as much as you do from the relationship. By using your sponsor, you are actually helping him or her in his or her recovery.

7. **If it doesn't work out.** You are always free to change your sponsor if you feel that the relationship is not giving you what you need.

Sponsorship or mentoring is a serious spiritual practice for those in recovery, both for those who are sponsored and those who sponsor. A Celtic saint, St. Brigit, put it best when she said, "Anyone without a soul friend is like a body without a head." What was true for Brigit in fifth century Ireland is all the more true for those of us trying to recover from addiction in a complex, fast-paced, and sometimes cynical modern world.

In Celtic spirituality there is a concept known as *anamchara* or soul friend. To be a soul friend is to provide a place of sanctuary to another where, through acceptance, love, and hospitality, he or she can grow in wisdom, and both of you in depth.

I've long regarded the idea of sponsorship to be a form of soul friendship. According to one of the experts on Celtic spirituality, soul friendships are characterized by six qualities, all of which can enhance recovery:

First, soul friendship is associated with great affection, intimacy, and depth.

Second, soul friend relationships are characterized by mutuality—a profound respect for each other's wisdom, despite any age or gender difference, and the awareness that the other person is a source of many blessings.

A third characteristic of soul friends is that they share common values and a common vision of reality.

Fourth, soul friendships include not only affirmation, but also the ability of each to challenge the other when necessary.

A fifth aspect of *anamchara* relationships is that they are centered on a Higher Power, the soul friend in whom all other friendships are united. True soul friends do not depend on each other alone, but root their relationship in God.

A sixth characteristic of soul friendship is that it survives geographical separation, the passage of time, and death itself. Soul friendship joins friends together in a common dwelling that neither time nor space nor death itself can separate—the dwelling of the soul and of the heart.

To be honest, I prefer the term "soul friend" to "sponsor." May we all find a soul friend. And may all of us who are called to be soul friends be blessed in our role as mentors and companions on the spiritual journey.

CHAPTER FIVE

Writing a Rule of Life

A Rule of Life is a written and articulated framework whereby we facilitate a regular pattern of spiritual formation. The term itself is derived from the Latin *regula*, which is the root of our English words *regular* and *regulation*. I realize that people, addicts especially, often hate the idea of being constrained by rules, but in this context a rule is self-imposed and personalized. Each person's rule is developed or adopted by that person and is devised by the author to regulate his or her life in a way that helps him or her grow. Paradoxically, while we hate regulations, we simultaneously yearn for regularity in our irregular lives. Following a Rule of Life, a regular discipline of spiritual growth, should become something we want to do in recovery. As someone once remarked, a Rule of Life is a tool for growth, not a pair of steel shackles.

The underlying premise of a Rule of Life is balance, with the divine as the center. A Rule of Life provides us with the direction we need to get on the path of real growth, and the loving accountability we need to keep us there.

For a long time, following a rule was something done only by those in monastic life. But in our own time, rules of life have been extended to all sorts of communities. Many people follow rules of life intended for communities such as communes, brotherhoods, and service organizations. I would argue, as an example, that the United States Marines follow a Rule of Life that is principled and disciplined, and they are hardly gentle monks. One might even say that in our twelve-step fellowships, the steps themselves constitute a Rule of Life that provides us with a set of principles to regulate our lives with decency and dignity.

Practicing a Rule of Life seems to move us against the grain of our individualistic culture and addictive natures, where we do what we want when we want. Despite this, many people develop rules that work for them or adopt rules devised by others that apply to them. In all cases, rules grow from the positive aspects of our life, not from what we perceive to be our failings. A Rule of Life should take us in the direction we want to go and the direction God wants us to go—hopefully those directions will be the same. A Rule of Life must be based in love.

As I mentioned in the Introduction, the granddaddy of all rules of life is the one developed in the sixth century by St. Benedict of Nursia for monks. Benedict was addressing the problem of how to regulate a group of men trying to live together in harmony and balance. To this end, he developed a simple Rule of Life that highlighted the importance of peace, prayer, work, sacrifice, humility, frugality, and obedience. His guidelines aided his monks in the pursuit of godliness and in learning how to relate to each other, to authority, and to guests. The underlying principles of the Benedictine Rule were stability, obedience, and conversion of life.

There are two things remarkable about the Benedictine Rule. First, it is quite simple and short. Second, it is still used today by Benedictines throughout the world. It is so successful that there are laypersons, some connected with Benedictine monasteries as oblates, others on their own, who try to adapt the Rule of Benedict for their everyday lives. For instance, there is a group of Episcopalians in Washington DC, who call themselves "The Friends of Benedict" who try to live according to the Rule. They organize Benedictine retreats and educate interested groups on Benedictine wisdom. They also sponsor ecumenical programs for clergy and lay people to explore the Rule of Benedict within a community of participants.

Here are some gems from the Rule of Benedict to give you an idea of how wise Benedict was about human nature:

"For monks who in a week's time say less than the full Book of Psalms with the customary canticles betray extreme indolence and lack of devotion in their service. We read, after all, that our holy fathers, energetic as they were, did all this in a single day. Let us hope that we, lukewarm as we are, can achieve it in a whole week." (18:24–25)

"We must know that God regards our purity of heart and tears of compunction, not our many words. Prayer should therefore be short and pure, unless perhaps it is prolonged under the inspiration of divine grace." (20:3–5)

"For nothing is so inconsistent with life as overindulgence." (39:8–9)

"Idleness is the enemy of the soul. Therefore, the brothers should have specified periods for manual labor as well as for prayerful reading." (48:1)

"When they live by the labor of their hands, as our fathers and the apostles did, then they are really monks. Yet, all things are to be done with moderation on account of the faint-hearted." (48:8–9)

"During the time of Lent each one is to receive a book from the library, and is to read the whole of it straight through. These books are to be distributed at the beginning of Lent." (48:15–16)

When you begin to look for them, rules of life abound. We don't have to go to monasteries to find them. All sorts of people are seeking simple principles by which to live their lives.

For instance, I am a member of the Rotary Club, which is an international service organization. I'm quite proud of my club, the Verrazano Rotary Club in

Brooklyn, which is noted for its breathtaking charity. At the end of each Rotary meeting we recite the Rotary "creed," known as the Four-Way Test, which asks us to examine the things we think, say, and do through these four questions: Is it true? Is it just to all involved? Will it create goodwill and improved friendships? And will it be beneficial to all involved?

One night while I was reciting the creed with others, I had an epiphany. Like all epiphanies it was painfully obvious. The Four-Way Test is actually a Rule of Life to those who follow it in their daily lives. How effectively this test reminds us to live daily in truth and justice, to strengthen the bonds of goodwill and friendship, and to do only those things that benefit all. The Four-Way Test meets all the criteria of a good Rule of Life. It is simple. It is godly. It is based in love. It allows persons to grow in virtue and in spirit.

So, how do you develop your own rule—that is, a rule that works for you, enhances your life, and honors where you are on your journey? It is important to remember that your rule is not going to be a statement of long-term goals about the person you aspire to be. It is not an ideal toward which you are striving. Your rule should be a realistic and manageable standard of how you want to manage your moral and spiritual life in terms of where you are now. When developing your rule remember the "HOW" you learned in the Second Step: honesty, open-mindedness, and willingness.

Adele Calhoun suggests that the rule you write should include three things: a self-assessment, an explanation of how you will practice your chosen disciplines, and your form of accountability.[15] First, she suggests that you come up with a clear self-evaluation that describes your current life circumstances, including your work and family responsibilities. Your self-assessment should include a reflection on the qualities of your character—your strengths and weaknesses. For instance, are you compassionate, self-controlled, or blessed with a spirit of joy? What temptations do you struggle with the most?

Of course, for persons in recovery, there is no better form of self-assessment available to us than our Fourth Step inventory and the face-to-face relating of it in the Fifth Step. This is a good time to ask your sponsor for candid feedback and about how you might develop a rule to guide you through your days. Beginning your rule with an honest self-assessment such as the Fourth Step will push you to develop a rhythm of life that is unique to your personality, circumstances, and needs.

Calhoun goes on to suggest that as a second step in developing your rule you should create a list of spiritual disciplines and practices that you can realistically make a part of your everyday life.[16] You should consider why your choices not only fit your situation in life but also how they address areas where you especially need discipline and growth. Making choices about specific disciplines require prayer and wisdom. As you decide on specific practices (for example, how and when to pray, serve, practice simplicity, etc.), consider the following questions:

- What disciplines and specific practices are you attracted to?
- Where do you sense that God is calling you to stretch and grow? Where do you want to change?
- In what areas of you life do you need more balance?
- If you could hear your own eulogy, what would you want to hear?
- Is your rule realistic for you to commit to?

The issue of accountability is the third and final step. Perhaps you have an *anamchara*, a spiritual friend and guide. That person could be your sponsor, your best friend, your partner, or your clergyperson. If your rule focuses on the ethics of your professional life, it could be a colleague. Do not fall into the trap of addictive thinking and believe you will be able to hold yourself accountable. We've all learned from painful experience that, as addicts in recovery, we need agents outside ourselves to monitor our lives and to tell us how we're doing. For me, one of the best benefits of accountability is having a sympathetic friend to help me when I'm stuck or when I've faltered or when I've been too stubborn to get out of a spiritual rut.

What Rule of Life do I follow? I try to follow two rules in my spiritual life, one individual and the other communal. The first is a short personal rule that I wrote myself. The second is a much longer rule that I have vowed to follow as a member of the religious order known as the Order of Urban Missioners.

First, here's my personal rule:

- I will maintain complete abstinence from all drugs.
- I will pray and meditate daily, seeking to discern God's will for me.
- I will serve others through membership in a twelve-step fellowship and through my ministry as a priest in the Episcopal Church.
- I will take a daily inventory of my behavior.
- I will receive the sacraments regularly, especially Holy Communion and the Reconciliation of a Penitent.
- I will maintain accountability through my sponsor, my confessor, my spiritual director, my home group, and my bishop.
- I will follow my physicians' orders.
- I will go on a retreat at least once a year.
- I will take a pilgrimage at least once a year.
- I will walk a half-hour every day.

The Order of Urban Missioners is a community of lay and ordained people who feel called to urban ministry and believe that a simple rule of spiritual discipline will help them to be faithful to that call. I first joined the order in the Diocese of Maryland in

2001 and currently serve the chapter in the Episcopal Diocese of New York as its Co-Convenor. For me, the Order has been a spiritual support group and source of solace and strength. I regularly attend its monthly chapter meetings that include a shared meal, prayers, silent meditation, and the Eucharist. I preach or celebrate mass for the members regularly and occasionally lead our meditations.

Our symbol is a cross within a circle within a square, representing God's love in the world and within the city block. To me, our symbol is reminiscent of various twelve-step logos. That similarity allows me to see the parallels between my various support groups and how they all mesh with my spiritual life.

I have covenanted in the presence of God and with my fellow members annually (usually in September) focusing on my call to ministry for the upcoming year. For instance, my vow for 2013 was the following: "To continue my service to addicts in recovery through sponsorship and writing and to be a good pastor to the people of St. Francis and St. Martha Parish where I am serving as interim priest." I regard my yearly vow to the Order as a mini-Rule of Life as it clarifies and makes specific my personal Rule of Life.

Last September I renewed my vows to the Order at the Cathedral of St. John the Divine. I have done this now for twelve years. Here is the rule I promised to follow to the best of my ability:

1. To give my fears and prejudices about urban living and ministry over to God.
2. To open myself to Christ's redeeming love, especially in the city.
3. To live in a state of love.

To this end, I vowed:

1. To take my calling to urban ministry seriously and to covenant with the Order yearly the location to which we feel called and the nature of that call.
2. To take care of my body, my mind, and my soul that I may be a useful instrument for God:
    a. To read and meditate on the Bible daily.
    b. To pray constantly, to pray for each other by name and to pray for Christ's work in the city.
    c. To make confession, receive spiritual direction, and spend time on retreats in a regular manner.
    d. To participate in worship, a daily office, and the Eucharist as often as possible.
    e. To take to heart the admonition in Ephesians to "put on the whole armor of God" (Ephesians 6:10–20).
    f. To take appropriate rest and time off, to exercise on a regular basis, and to eat properly.
3. To support each other in our various callings:
    a. To gather together for Eucharist on a regular basis.

b. To share my story for mutual support, guidance, and for the increase of my faith.

c. To sing together whenever possible as a joyful way to send the demons scurrying.

d. To share in educational programs appropriate to our needs and ministries.

4. To commit myself to good works and acts of love, and to allow that God will bless me and change me through this calling:

a. To treat all people equally as God's people.

b. To listen to God's people and to be open to new ways of sharing Christ's love.

c. To wear a visible sign of our Order.

A saying I hear around the rooms of recovery is that "spiritual principles are never in conflict." I know from my own life that this is true. To the best of my ability I follow my own Rule of Life, the Rule of the Order of Urban Missioners, the vows I've taken as a priest, and the Twelve Steps. All of them are compatible. None of them conflict with each other. Each of them enriches my life, advances my recovery, and facilitates my spiritual growth.

A Prayer for the Suffering Addict

REV. JOHN T. FARRELL

Essence of Love, bestow your spirit on those addicts who are in despair. Comfort them, in their time of pain, and relieve them of their isolation. Cast away from them the specter of despair and destruction that enfolds them. Help them that they may be free from the shackles of addiction. Let them come to know that life is precious and recovery is a gift to be nurtured. Remember and help all addicts who suffer, in and out of the rooms of recovery, and keep them in your heart.

From *Guide Me in My Recovery: Prayers for Times of Joy and Times of Trial* by The Reverend John T. Farrell, PhD. © 2010 Central Recovery Press.

CHAPTER SIX

Lectio Divina

Part of the recovery process for many of us involves reading, especially program literature. Stories abound of how in the early days of the twelve-step movement people would find recovery through reading the Big Book. As a sponsor of newcomers I often ask them to read certain chapters in the Basic Text or *It Works: How and Why*. Efforts have been made to translate literature into as many languages as possible so addicts throughout the world can share in the wealth of the written word. These days, my favorite meetings are those that read and then discuss program literature. The written word resonates very deeply with us. Our literature is a permanent record of distilled wisdom and shared experience. It's one of the cornerstones of many people's recoveries.

After a while, many of us expand our reading horizons and seek out other forms of literature to enhance our recoveries. Accordingly, we read day-by-day meditation books. We read spiritual classics.

We read self-help books. We read the sacred scriptures of various religions. We read spiritual autobiographies. I personally also find enlightenment and spiritual depth in certain kinds of poetry.

There is a method of reading that has helped me in appreciating its full spiritual value. This method or technique is called *lectio divina*, which is Latin for "sacred reading." In its classic form, *lectio divina* was confined to the slow perusal of sacred scripture, both the Old and New Testaments. It was initially undertaken by monks, not with the intention of gaining information, but of using the texts as an aide to contact the living God. In our time, the spiritual practice of *lectio* can be employed for just about any type of spiritual reading. Basic to the practice of *lectio divina* is a desire to connect with a Higher Power and to grow spiritually. This sense of connection and growth is sustained by further reading, so as we continue, we are actually growing and deepening our spiritual discernment.

There are various ways to practice *lectio* and I shall recommend one that I think will work best for people in recovery. The crucial point is that practitioners must resist the temptation to cover a given amount of material within a prescribed time frame. So if you've taken a speed-reading course (which I have), you need to forget what you've learned. Reading things quickly, skimming them, and trying to summarize are part of our culture, which has been alternately blessed and cursed by an information explosion that mandates quick reading. In *lectio divina* we are asked to slow down, ponder, even linger over particular words or phrases. We have a lifetime to grow spiritually, so take it easy and prepare yourself to smell the roses.

It was an eleventh-century monk named Guigo who first wrote down the steps used in *lectio divina,* which he called *The Stairway to Heaven.* Since then the method has always followed the same general pattern. For Guigo, the method involved four steps or rungs on a ladder. Those steps, and Guigo's brief descriptions of them, are:

1. **Lectio** (reading): "Looking on Holy Scripture with all one's will and wit."
2. **Meditatio** (meditation): "A studious searching with the mind to know what was before concealed through desiring proper skill."
3. **Oratio** (prayer): "A devout desiring of the heart to get what is good and avoid what is evil."
4. **Contemplatio** (contemplation): "The lifting up of the heart to God tasting somewhat of the heavenly sweetness and savor."

In more modern terms, here is my interpretation of the steps that I use for myself and would recommend to you.

• I always begin by saying this prayer: "May I be fully alive to the holy presence as I leave my tasks and worries. May I be enfolded in love, find rest, and discover enlightenment. Let my heart become one with the universe. *Amen.*"

- **Reading** (*lectio*): The first order of business is to select a text. Later on in this chapter I'll make some recommendations that will help get you started. An important thing to remember is that program literature is always appropriate for *lectio divina*. Be prepared for doing some basic literary analysis as you read—that is, look at the reading's context and origin, the author's intent and your expectations, the words and images used to convey the point, how the characters operate, and the literary form and structure employed. Decide how much you're going to read. Read the selection slowly, savoring every word. Don't be afraid to read something a second time, even a third.

- **Meditation** (*meditatio*): Pause in your reading and take into account the content of the passage and your own dispositions. What are the themes in the reading? How do they relate to you and your life? What this text will say to you will also depend to some extent on your state of mind and soul as you read it. You may be weary, frustrated, and depressed, and badly in need of rest. Or you may be feeling fabulous, seeking a spiritual breakthrough. Factor your own feelings into how the reading touches you.

- **Prayer** (*oratio*): This flows from reading and meditating on the text. This step, of course, is very personal. I may ask God to help me find serenity and peace of mind. Or I may thank God for the gift of my recovery. I always pray for suffering addicts in and out of the rooms who could benefit from reading what I have just read.

- **Contemplation** (*contemplatio*): This involves relishing the spiritual experience and praising God for it. It is a way of bringing the prayer experience to closure, always ending on a note of gratitude.

- **Action** (*actio*): Here I discern a course of action. I promise myself to do this again. I determine to grow in virtue. I will try to be a better sponsor. I may feel a need for something deeper and decide to make a retreat or to pray more regularly. I definitely try to understand how to better live and work.

As I stated before, using this method of slow reading, prayer, and meditation enhances program literature, so that's always a good place to start trying the technique. But beyond the books we all know, there's a vast library of accessible and useful spiritual resources that can be used as part of a program of *lectio divina*. Here are ten suggestions for books that I have used and can highly recommend:

The Wounded Healer by Henri Nouwen. This author was one of my great spiritual inspirations. In this,

his classic work, he develops a balanced and creative theology of service that begins with the realization of fundamental woundedness in human nature. He sees our woundedness as a source of strength and healing when serving others. We live in a suffering world, are part of a suffering generation, are suffering persons ourselves, and are committed to helping suffering addicts. Nouwen believes we must recognize our own suffering and make that recognition the starting point of our service. To that end, we must be willing to go beyond detached charity and leave ourselves open as fellow human beings with the wounds and suffering of others. In other words, we heal from our own wounds. Or as we say in the rooms of recovery, "We keep what we have by giving it away."

Of Character by Denise Crosson. This is a reflective narrative discussing topics on building and practicing character assets. Dr. Crosson uses quotes from various sources to describe how the principles embodied in the Twelve Steps can enrich an individual's life. She offers a fresh perspective on topics such as commitment, devotion, forgiveness, and integrity, to name but a few.

No Man Is an Island by Thomas Merton is one of the most popular of this spiritual giant's thirty books. Here he provides meditations on the spiritual life in sixteen thoughtful essays, beginning with his classic treatise, "Love Can Be Kept Only by Being Given Away." The essays provide insight into Merton's favorite topics of silence and solitude, while also underscoring the importance of community and the deep connectedness to others that is the inevitable basis of the spiritual life—whether one lives in solitude or in the midst of a crowd.

Gay Spirituality by Toby Johnson offers a sensible, modern, and enlightened understanding of spiritual consciousness for gay men who are so often faced with misunderstanding and conflict dealing with traditional religion. It envisions a world where same-sex love is recognized as a face of spirit, intrinsic to human nature, and a path to liberation. *Gay Spirituality* is an important resource for LGBTQ addicts seeking to reconcile their sexual orientation with their spirituality and with their new life of recovery.

The Gift of Years by Joan Chittister addresses aging—an issue that is close to my heart. As I write this, I have just celebrated thirty-eight years of recovery. I came into the program when I was twenty-seven; now I'm sixty-five. Long-term recovery, in my case, equals old age. Chittister looks at the many facets of the aging process, from its challenges and struggles to its joys and surprises. Central throughout is a call to cherish the blessing of aging as a natural part of life that is active, productive, and deeply rewarding. There is a purpose to aging and a specific intention is built into every stage of life. Chittister reflects on many key issues, including the temptation toward isolation, the need to stay involved, the importance of health and well-being, what happens when old relationships end or shift, the fear of tomorrow, and the mystery of forever. There is beauty in aging, as I am finding out myself.

There are many day-by-day meditations to choose from, but *Just for Today* is a classic, written by addicts for addicts. There are 365 daily meditations, each focused on a specific recovery theme. Each page begins with a pertinent quote from recovery literature to set the stage, followed by a brief meditation on the topic, and ending with a brief prayer whose opening is always the same, "Just for today . . . ."

Plain Living by Catherine Whitmire focuses on and provides direction to the gimmick-free spiritual path followed by Quakers. For over three centuries Quakers have been living out of a spiritual center in a way of life they call "plain living." Their accumulated experiences and distilled wisdom have much to offer anyone seeking greater simplicity in our world today. *Plain Living* is not about sacrifice. It's about choosing the life you really want, a form of inward simplicity that leads us to listen for the "still, small voice" of God.

Wise Women by Susan Neunzig Cahill assembles a representative sample of the worldwide breadth of women's spirituality. Cahill has selected some ninety writings encompassing a wide variety of faiths and traditions. The writings contain profound moments of conversion and intense epiphanies of personal revelation from authors as wide-ranging as Sappho, Julian of

Norwich, Teresa of Avila, Sun Bu'er, Mechthild of Magdeburg, Mirabai, Dorothy Sayers, Hannah Arendt, Iris Murdoch, Denise Levertov, Lucille Clifton, and Marge Piercy. The result is a very satisfying anthology, illuminating and useful, that can be appreciated by both women and men seeking new voices on their spiritual journeys.

Leaves of Grass by Walt Whitman first opened my eyes to spirituality in my early recovery. I was studying it for a graduate seminar and became enthralled by Whitman's vision of a universal spirituality of connectedness and community when he proclaimed, "I am you and you are me." After years of depression, isolation, and despair, the optimism of Whitman's poetry set me on a new path of hope and love. Paradoxically, Whitman also emphasized my uniqueness and the courage I would need to walk life's journey:

> "Not I, nor anyone else can travel
>   that road for you.
> You must travel it by yourself.
> It is not far. It is within reach.
> Perhaps you have been on it since you
>   were born, and did not know.
> Perhaps it is everywhere—
>   on water and land."

If you're interested in pursuing *lectio divina* with poetry, I would also recommend John Donne.

The Celtic Vision edited by Esther de Waal. If you're in need of a book of prayers, this rich array includes elements that address every side of life—hearth, home, work, and play—to sanctify human endeavor. You don't have to be Irish to find something that will resonate in your life.

SOUGHT
THROUGH
PRAYER AND
MEDITATION

CHAPTER SEVEN

Rituals

It may seem odd that there would be a chapter on "ritual" in a book on spiritual practices. We live in an age where informality is the rule and ritual is suspect. Many of us associate ritual with religious practices we have abandoned. Stripped of connotations, however, a ritual is very simply anything we do repeatedly or do in a particular manner. I can say it is my morning ritual to get a cup of coffee soon after waking up. I sorely miss it if I don't do it every morning. I can say that it has become a family ritual to eat our holiday meals at about 4:00 P.M., after an afternoon of watching football.

In fact, ritual is a large part of our lives in recovery programs. For example, we ritualistically welcome newcomers to our meetings with shouts of encouragement and offers of phone numbers. We celebrate anniversaries as rituals with cakes and special meeting formats. We gather in conventions to enjoy each other's company, culminating in the grand ritual called the "recovery countdown."

We tell our stories as part of the ritual of meetings. We follow daily routines of prayer and meditation. We revel in the transformation of others' lives and reach out to the poor guy who doesn't introduce himself by saying, "I'm John and I'm an _____." All of these are rituals that are crucial to recovery.

However, we rarely call these things "rituals" because the term itself is viewed with suspicion—a bias that unfortunately carries over into our spiritual lives. Many people believe that "empty" should always be used to qualify the word "ritual." To me, that attitude speaks volumes about a certain understanding of the world in which we live and the nature of our relationship to powers greater than ourselves. Time and experience have given me a radically different take on ritual—both on what it really is, and on the place it holds in our world. Ritual is not only *not* empty— often it is the bearer of fullness. It is a spiritual practice that should be reckoned with.

Where does our dislike of ritual come from? Let's look at history, especially the history of Christianity. Whether we are religious or not, the history of Western culture affects our attitudes and our lives. For instance, the arguments that arose from the Protestant Reformation have had a dramatic impact on the surrounding culture. Among those arguments was a new view of ritual as it played out in people's lives. Reformers like Luther, Calvin, and Cranmer were not enemies of liturgy: their reformed communities continued to worship with "reformed" liturgies. But the central acts of ceremony were radically changed and there was a move away from ritual acts.

The anti-ritual of the Reformation is rooted in a worldview that I find prevalent in our secular society today. Ritual acts are regarded as "empty" and "meaningless." The word "spiritual" has come to be identified with internal, mental, interior acts of the heart. To be spiritual in many minds is to be spontaneous, original, and individual. Many people in the program distrust ritual as part of doctrine and dogma.

The beginnings of this worldview are rooted in the dialectical opposition of faith and works. In Reformation shorthand, faith is good and works are bad. Faith becomes synonymous with certain *mental* acts. Works became associated with almost every outward action. Even almsgiving came to be seen as a "work." With the "interiorizing" of all things spiritual, ritual actions became virtually demonized (hence "empty ritual"). Indeed, some began to view any use of ritual as, in fact, demonic ("witchcraft"). Priests became worse than heretics—they were viewed as *necromancers* and the like.

Of course, the extremes of argumentation rarely make for useful reflection (consider modern political "discussion" and the low-level discourse that has dominated the last several presidential elections). Hence, the exact nature of ritual never comes up as a topic worthy of consideration. Is there a good use of ritual? What would make it good or bad? I would like to suggest several possible ways to see ritual as a positive activity that can enhance spiritual growth and personal recovery.

One positive way to view ritual is to perceive it as a *mental* construct. What something means is what someone *thinks* it means. The task of ritual then is to help each other see and understand meaning. In such an understanding, everything of value that takes place in rituals occurs within someone's mind. Bodies, light, color, sound, bread, statues, icons, candles, smell, text, etc. are incidental: they only have value because they create the occasion for thought. "Spiritual" and "mental," then, are two words for the same thing.

Another way to understand ritual is to invest it with deeper meaning and to actually think something is happening in ritualistic actions—something that is not just an event in someone's mind. In this sense, the rituals we perform don't lead us *to* something, they *are* something.

So what then does ritual really do? One answer is that it does just what it appears to do. Ritual actions are iconic in nature—they make present that which they represent. Thus, in religious terms, to make the sign of the cross in blessing yourself is to bless yourself. Or, to put it in program terms, to attempt to call a friend in recovery is as useful to our recoveries as actually getting through to the other person. We do with our bodies what we say with our lips (and often more).

Rituals also offer deep comfort because of their familiarity and repetition. When I am distressed, I go to a meeting. Believing, however, that meetings are places where recovery is discussed and learned, I usually do not share my misery or despair. People aren't interested, I reason, in my drama and trauma; they're here for something positive. Instead, I listen. Often just sitting there, hearing the readings, and being in the company of people who love and understand me soothes and calms me. The familiar rituals of the meeting offer me solace and a sense that the world is still turning and that people seeking and finding recovery are my priority. The rituals of the meeting bring me far more peace than any outpouring of negative emotion ever did. It's the ritual—the atmosphere of recovery, if you will—that centers me.

As for those who simply oppose all ritual—they take an absurd position. Human beings have bodies and they move, speak, touch, hear, and smell. Those movements have always been understood to carry meaning. When you think about it, twelve-step fellowships are filled with rituals that carry great meaning for their members. At my home group, we start on time with the same readings each Saturday. We read a welcoming statement written by the home group members. After hearing a speaker discuss a topic, we open the floor for sharing. Like many meetings in New York we use a timer so no one can "hold the meeting hostage" by self-centered rambling. The meeting ends promptly after an hour. We join in a circle to say the Third Step and Serenity Prayers to conclude. These are our rituals. They comfort and support us. They speak to our recovery. It wouldn't be our meeting without them. We would be uncomfortable if they were violated or denigrated.

There is no empty ritual, for there is no empty action. Everything is filled with meaning and power. Sometimes for good. We should all consciously incorporate rituals into our lives. They promote stability and keep us grounded. They have the potential to fill our lives with meaning. Here are some suggestions for daily, personal rituals that can help people in their recoveries.

Create a Personal Quiet Space for Prayer and Meditation

The whole purpose of this book is to help you work Step Eleven, that is, pray and meditate. Praying itself is a ritual. Praying at a regular time and in a regular order adds more ritual, as does praying in a regular space that has been prepared for that purpose.

The Gospel of Matthew offers good advice about the value of having a personal space for prayer. The author tells us that "Whenever you pray, go into your room and shut the door and pray to your Father who is in secret; and your Father who sees in secret will reward you" (6:6).

To determine your own personal place may require some creativity depending on your living situation. In a large home you can designate a spare room. In a small house or apartment a corner in the bedroom or the living room may be the ideal place. In a dorm room you could use your desk. A creative use of a bookcase can also help to create a private nook. Designing it is something that requires serious thought, as this space becomes a sacred place in the midst of your living space.

Some people who take their living environments seriously use the principles of feng shui to design their prayer spaces and often their whole homes. Feng shui is an ancient art and science developed over 3,000 years ago in China. It is a complex body of knowledge that reveals how to balance the energies of any given space to assure health and good fortune for people inhabiting it. Feng shui is rooted in the yin yang theory, which is one of the central concepts in all ancient Chinese thought. Traditional Chinese Medicine, ancient martial arts, feng shui, the I Ching, and the whole Taoist cosmology are all based on the dynamics of yin and yang. According to this theory, everything in our universe is composed of two opposing, but deeply interconnected forces—the yin (feminine) and the yang (masculine). The interaction of these two feng shui forces creates the essence of life around us. One cannot exist without the other, as in their seeming opposition they deeply support and nourish each other.

Feng shui is not for the untrained. Although some levels of feng shui are easy to understand and apply, the core knowledge takes years of study. Just like Traditional Chinese Medicine, feng shui knowledge is deep and complex. The more you know about feng shui, the more you realize how much more there is to explore. But there are many resources available in bookstores and online that will help you choose colors, arrange furniture, hang pictures, and use decorations.

To design your sacred space for personal rituals, begin by arranging the room simply. Next, bring into the room symbols for what you hold sacred: emblems of your spirituality, religious images, figures, or scriptures that you hold dear. You can use artifacts from your program of recovery. Find a dresser top or small table on which to display them, and let that be your altar—a special setting for your sacred objects.

At my house I have a comfortable chair that looks out over the Hudson River and the Palisades, a set of spectacular cliffs. Next to the chair is a table with a candle and a Lucite case displaying my recovery medallion. Hanging nearby is an antique icon from the Russian Orthodox Church. These surroundings represent enlightenment, nature, recovery, and God. Several times a day I sit my chair, light my candle, play ambient music, breathe deeply, and read from one of several meditation books. Then I sit and focus on one theme that attracted me in my reading. At some point I just sit and listen for the still, small voice of my Higher Power. That is my prayer ritual in my sacred space.

Worship

Religious worship as a spiritual practice is not something everyone enjoys. I personally do and see great value in the rituals of organized religion. If you are a churchgoer or decide to attend church (or temple or synagogue or mosque or sacred grove) you are entering a world of ritual that has developed time-tested methods for connecting with God. Worship allows you to engage with others in focused prayer, in song, and in shared belief. It connects you with a fellowship of believers who will often invite you to join them in acts of charity and in helping others as part of their expressions of faith and growing in virtue. Most of all, you will discover and learn rituals that are designed to help you feel God's presence and to understand how God acts in your life and recovery. Some churches also offer rituals that will help you feel forgiven for the wreckage of your past and look forward to your new life in recovery as a productive member of society.

Sharing Food

Preparing and eating meals together and sharing the art of cooking can be rituals that brighten our lives and refresh our souls.

When I was a boy I had four aunts who had never married. They all lived in the house in which they were born. Three of them pursued careers while the fourth sister remained home to keep house and tend to my grandmother who passed away when I was six. Visiting my aunts was a monthly treat, and it was filled with little rituals that I eagerly looked forward to. One aunt would buy my brothers and me comic books and hide them in the same place for us to find. Upon leaving, each would give us a quarter, except my Aunt Luanna who would ask, "How much did the others give you?" Thereupon she gave us each a dollar. Driving home, my mother would always demand, "Did Luanna give you any money?" And we'd say, "She said not to tell you."

My favorite ritual of all was watching my Aunt Helen in the late afternoon bake the best oatmeal cookies in the world from scratch. We'd watch entranced as she mixed the cookie dough, arguing over who would get to lick the bowl and spoon. Then she put them in the oven and we'd wait until they were ready to eat—warm oatmeal cookies with cold milk.

Years later, when I was clearing out family memorabilia I found Helen's recipe for oatmeal cookies. I've baked them myself, but they never taste the same as they did back in Helen's kitchen in the 1950s. I'm lacking the essential ingredient: love and three special little boys to eat them. In any case, you may wish to try your luck.

AUNT HELEN'S SUPER
OATMEAL COOKIES

1¾ cups old-fashioned rolled oats

¾ cup all-purpose flour

¾ teaspoon cinnamon

½ teaspoon baking soda

½ teaspoon salt

1¼ sticks unsalted butter, softened

⅓ cup packed light brown sugar

⅓ cup granulated sugar

1 large egg

½ teaspoon vanilla

Preheat oven to 375°F. Grease baking sheets.

Stir together oats, flour, cinnamon, baking soda, and salt. Beat together butter, brown sugar, and granulated sugar in a large bowl with an electric mixer until light and fluffy. Add egg and vanilla and beat until combined well. Add oat mixture and beat until just combined.

Drop dough by heaping tablespoons two inches apart onto baking sheets and flatten mounds slightly with moistened fingers. Bake cookies in upper and lower thirds of oven, switching position of sheets halfway through baking, until golden, about twelve minutes total. Transfer to racks to cool.

Rites of Passage

Within the realm of personal rituals, rites of passage are also an important part of how our society functions. We all celebrate and commemorate common rites of passage, like birth, graduation, marriage, and death. In recovery we celebrate our anniversaries, which are important rituals in our community. But we also tend to overlook other rites of passage. Some rites of passage that I think are quite often neglected are the smaller events that are nonetheless meaningful in our lives, especially the milestones in our new lives of recovery—events such as learning to drive a car, voting for the first time, getting a raise, having our children returned to us because we are no longer a danger to them and our recoveries are recognized as lasting, being taken off probation, going back to school, obtaining a GED, reuniting with an estranged family member, and finding a better job.

Our minds need to be able to celebrate the small events as well as the big events in our lives to feel connected. So, when something good happens to you, develop a ritual for celebration—say a prayer of gratitude, go to a meeting, or take your sponsor to dinner and thank him or her for believing in you.

Acts of Kindness and Charity

Addiction is a disease of self-absorption and relating to others unselfishly is often not natural to us. One way to escape the bondage of self is to develop rituals of kindness that are consistent and habitual. When we feel love and kindness toward others, it not only makes others feel loved and cared for, but it also helps us to develop inner happiness and peace. It certainly helps us in our recovery by becoming better people, but sometimes practicing kindness can help us overcome our character defects as well. Love and kindness can also aid us when we are depressed, as the writer Sarah Fielding observed, "The words of kindness are more healing to a drooping heart than balm or honey."

Let me give you an example of how a ritual of kindness can do these things: I can be an angry, impatient driver. Maybe it's a reaction to stress, perhaps it's a lingering sense of addictive entitlement, but I can be a master of angry gestures and horn honking when I am crossed, literally and figuratively, on the road.

One day I had an epiphany. I was wearing my clerical collar when someone cut me off on I-95 in Wilmington, Delaware. I was outraged! To put it bluntly, I gave him the finger, flipped him the bird, threw him the one-finger salute. The other person saw how I was dressed and looked shocked. I realized who I was—a priest in recovery—and was ashamed of myself.

I determined not to let that happen again. But how? An answer came to me through a group called the Episcopal Church Women (ECW). At about that time the women of the ECW in my parish were distributing collection boxes to Episcopalians throughout the US. People drop a bit of small change into the box as a thanksgiving for an event (however small) in their lives. The funds collected through this effort, called the United Thank Offering, are substantial, and help to fund a variety of efforts worldwide, such as disaster relief, medical aid, and scholarships.

Since that day in 1992 in Wilmington, I have kept a United Thank Offering box in my car. Every time I feel angry with another driver and don't show it, I thank God and donate a dollar to the box. If I do act in an unseemly manner, I fine myself five dollars. This ritual has, over the last twenty years, made me a better driver and a better person. The five dollar fines are rare and far-between these days, and I attribute that to my little ritual of safe driving, charity, and recovery.

There are many ways to develop rituals of kindness in your own life. The Random Acts of Kindness Foundation lists 273 ideas on its webpage.[17] Here are just a few:

- Cleaning up graffiti and other signs of vandalism in your area or a poorer neighborhood nearby is a great way of giving back to your community.
- Bring books to your local library or community organization. A lot of children don't have access to books for lack of funds or because their families are in no position to value education.

- Stop to help when you see someone in need. Be it a broken down car, or a child wandering about who is looking for its parents, or a person who is visibly in distress. Of course be careful and always use precaution and good judgment when approaching strangers. But also trust your empathic abilities and remember that the feeling of being stranded somewhere, lost, or upset in public can be extremely stressful, and also very lonely. All it might take to boost someone's spirits is for someone to stop and see if there is anything they can help with. Even if help is already on the way, he or she will be grateful for your gesture.

- Hold the door. Holding the door open is a considerate act you can easily do for your family, friends, and strangers, every day. Even small gestures of care and thoughtfulness go a long way, and whether you're at a store, at school, at work, or at home, anyone around you will certainly appreciate your good manners.

- Let someone go ahead of you. Almost every day we find ourselves in situations where we are required to wait in line—something that causes many people to become irritable and impatient. This applies especially to driving, where letting another driver go in front of you when they need to change lanes or make a turn can make a really big difference. Being patient and letting someone in brings ease into a tense situation, and can end up making a person's day a little bit better.

- Pick up trash. Make your surroundings more beautiful! Be kind to the environment and those around you by picking up trash when you see it lying around. It doesn't matter who left it there, just pick it up!

CHAPTER EIGHT ·

Pilgrimage

Throughout history people of various backgrounds and beliefs have embraced the spiritual practice of pilgrimage by journeying to sacred places or shrines of special beauty, spirituality, or significance. This outward journey to a *place* paralleled an inner, spiritual journey of the *soul*. The act of pilgrimage was meant to probe deep human emotions and longings.

I have always been fascinated by the concept of pilgrimage. Perhaps it's my Celtic heritage, but even before I knew the terminology, I sensed that some places were holier than others and that some places uplifted my soul. There were also places that I knew would bring me feelings of serenity, peace, and well-being— just as there were places that seemed malignant and filled with negative energy. The positive places I sensed, I came to realize, must be the "thin places" of Celtic spirituality, places where the world of the divine and the realm of matter are very close.

The first time I realized that pilgrimage—going to a "thin place" to find peace—could help me on my journey of recovery was in the mid-1980s when I had an unexpected and devastating professional setback. I was removed from a university administrative position as a result of academic politics, not because of my competence. I loved the job and felt the injustice deeply and personally. That the news was delivered to me bluntly, and without regard to my feelings, did not help matters.

That day, I left my department chair's office utterly devastated. It was a beautiful spring day and I took a walk around campus. I was on the faculty of an urban university with lots of unexpected nooks and crannies. I eventually came to an out-of-the-way garden that was usually deserted and overlooked. As I sat on a bench (and maybe cried a bit) I began to feel a sense of calm. I prayed and eventually I felt both my body and my mind relax. I began to think more clearly about what had happened to me and about who I was. I realized the chair's decision to remove me as the center's director didn't reflect upon my skills or me. That decision was outside of me and I was powerless over it. Despite the setback, I was still the intelligent, competent person I was when I had gone to work that day. Nothing had changed me. Life was filled with setbacks anyway. It was my task to rise to the challenge and prevail. And so I did.

What I had experienced was a pilgrimage, a journey, however short, to a place of repose and spiritual renewal that refreshed me and enabled me to return to my world ready to face life on life's terms. Would I have recovered emotionally as quickly as I did had I not gone into that garden? Who knows? I do know that whatever happened worked. I went into the garden broken and bereft. I returned whole and strong.

Pilgrimages are an old form of spiritual seeking. For several thousand years people of all faiths and of no faith have embarked on the practice of pilgrimage by journeying to a sacred place or shrine of special significance. This outward journey of movement and energy is accompanied by an inner, spiritual journey. All major religions have a concept and practice of pilgrimage that fills both individual and communal needs.

Pilgrimages were widely known and recorded in the ancient world. The Romans and Greeks flocked to the Oracle at Delphi, for instance. Several of the so-called Seven Wonders of the Ancient World—the Temple of Artemis at Ephesus, the Statue of Zeus in Greece, the Mausoleum at Halicarnassus in Turkey, and the Colossus of Rhodes—were sacred places of pilgrimage as well.

The Jewish people practiced pilgrimage too. Both agricultural festivals and historical events in the history of the Jewish people are described in the Hebrew Bible and are still celebrated. Three holidays in particular (Passover, Shavuot, and Sukkot) were set aside in biblical times for people to travel to the ancient Temple in Jerusalem on pilgrimage. Today, Jews from all over the world gather in Jerusalem and at the Wailing Wall.

The Buddha himself specified places of pilgrimage and their spiritual value. In the *Mahaparinibbana Sutta*, he enumerates four places that can bring about feelings of religious awe and repentance and are therefore worthy places of pilgrimage for those who believe in his precepts. These places include: where he was born (Lumbini), where he attained the enlightenment (Buddhagaya), where he delivered the first sermon (Sarnath), and where he entered into Mahaparinirvana or Nirvana (Kushinagar). Buddhists also travel to various sacred cities and shrines as well.

For Hindus, the purpose of a pilgrimage is *darsan*, that is, standing in the presence of a deity and looking upon the image with their eyes. To do so is to see, be seen, and be blessed. Pilgrims from all over the world travel to India to visit holy sites, known as *tirthas*. There they also seek the *darsan* of the places where they believe gods have dwelled. Sites near the Ganges River are the most popular for pilgrims.

In Islam, pilgrimage is viewed as a spiritual requirement. The *Hajj* (pilgrimage to Mecca) is the fifth of the fundamental Muslim practices and institutions known as the five pillars of Islam. For Muslims, pilgrimage is seen as a meritorious activity and serves as a penance, forgiveness for sins, devotion, and spiritual growth. And while not required, there are other Islamic sites of pilgrimage, most notably Medina and Jerusalem.

Christians have practiced pilgrimage almost from their beginnings. By the fourth century, Jerusalem had become a Christianized city and a focal point of pilgrimage. There is a fascinating account of one such journey known as *The Pilgrimage of Egeria*, written in 384 AD (available online for anyone who is interested). In many ways Egeria set the pattern for future pilgrimages. She introduced a devotional approach that highly valued relics and artifacts used by holy people, where one felt spiritually uplifted at the mere presence of a holy site, and learned the importance of reflecting on, and learning from, the sacred events that took place there.

As Christianity grew and spread, and as time passed, more and more sites became places of pilgrimage. Particularly in the Middle Ages, people in the Western world saw pilgrimage as a sacred duty. Since Jerusalem was no longer accessible to most, numerous other sites became places of veneration. Probably the most famous in the English-speaking world was the shrine of Thomas à Becket of Canterbury, made immortal by Geoffrey Chaucer's *The Canterbury Tales*. Some of us may remember having to memorize the opening to the Prologue in Middle English when we were in school:

> *Whan that Aprille with his shoures soote*
> *The droghte of Marche hath perced to the roote,*

And bathed every veyne in swich licour,

Of which vertu engendred is the flour;

Whan Zephirus eek with his swete breeth

Inspired hath in every holt and heeth

The tendre croppes, and the yonge sonne

Hath in the Ram his halfe cours y-ronne,

And smale fowles maken melodye,

That slepen al the night with open ye,

(So priketh hem nature in hir corages):

Than longen folk to goon on pilgrimages,

And palmers for to seken straunge strondes,

To ferne halwes, couthe in sondry londes;

And specially, from every shires ende

Of Engelond, to Caunterbury they wende,

The holy blisful martir for to seke,

That hem hath holpen, whan that they were seke.

In modern, nonpoetical English this passage means, *In the springtime, many people are inspired to go on religious pilgrimages to holy places. Their motivation to roam is great. The April rains have soaked deep into the dry ground to water the flowers' roots. Zephyrus, the god of the West wind, has helped new flowers to grow everywhere. Not only that, you can also see the constellation Aries in the sky. And, most importantly, the birds are singing all the time. You can go to other countries, but many English people in England choose to go to the city of Canterbury in southeastern England to*

*visit the remains of Thomas Becket, the Christian martyr
who had the power of healing people.*

I want to answer a question I can imagine some
of my readers asking—yelling even. "Are pilgrimages
all about religion? Does one have to follow a particular
faith to reap any benefit?" The answer to that question is
a twofold "no." First, there are many secular pilgrimage
sites. And second, some sites, while religious in origin,
have a universal spiritual appeal.

To expand on the first "no." Different places have
different meanings for different people. A pilgrimage
could be a visit to Graceland, the house in Memphis
where Elvis lived, or to Umberto's Clam House, the
restaurant where Joey Gallo ate his last meal; it could be
an attempt to retrace a leg of Captain Bligh's expedition
or peeking in at the Stonewall, the bar where the gay
rights movement began. In the twelve-step world we have
a number of sacred venues. People can visit Bill Wilson's
house, Stepping Stones, in New York. In 2012, Dr. Bob
Smith's house in Akron, Ohio, was designated a National
Landmark. People flock to find sites associated with the
founding of the twelve-step movement. Someone even
compiled a list to visit the graves of the first one hundred
members of AA. In Narcotics Anonymous, people travel
to see the location of the first NA meeting in Sun Valley,
California, or to visit the grave of Danny Carlson, an NA
predecessor who died in the 1950s, in Queens, New York.
All of these are examples of nonreligious pilgrimages.

Let me give you an example of the second "no"—places that have universal appeal beyond religion. People in recovery like to visit Calvary Episcopal Church on Park Avenue South in Manhattan as a place of pilgrimage. Its value for them doesn't derive from the fact that it's a religious building, but because The Rev. Dr. Samuel Shoemaker was the rector (pastor) there in the 1930s. It was in this building that Bill Wilson frequently consulted Shoemaker on spiritual matters, becoming so influenced by him that he named Father Shoemaker a "co-founder of Alcoholics Anonymous." Shoemaker is currently being considered for canonization in the Episcopal Church. His feast day is January 31 and the prayer for that day expresses thanks to God for the vision of Samuel Shoemaker and the hope that we may follow his example to reach out to others and be of service.

Pilgrimages have been an enormous help to me in my recovery. I undertake two types of pilgrimage: The first are ones I can take in my backyard, like the garden I described at the beginning of the chapter, and ones I can visit in a day or during part of a day. Then there are the ones I actually have to travel a distance to get to. For the purpose of providing examples, I'm going to give you lists of both types of pilgrimages that have helped me. The first focuses on New York City, which is where I live. Use these for inspiration to create your own list of special places in your neighborhood—all towns and cities have places comparable to the ones I describe. The second set of examples is partially a bucket list of places all around the world I hope to visit before I die. Some I've seen, others are still waiting for me. My cardiologist, however, has told me that one in particular, Machu Picchu, will have to wait until I've lost fifty pounds!

Backyard Pilgrimages in the New York Area

The Cloisters are a museum and gardens on the northern tip of Manhattan. The museum was assembled from architectural elements, both domestic and religious, that date from the twelfth through the fifteenth century. It has magnificent views and a sense of serenity throughout. I often take a book and go and read there during the afternoon.

The Japanese Hill-and-Pond Garden at the Brooklyn Botanic Gardens is one of the oldest and most visited Japanese-inspired gardens outside Japan. It is a blend of the ancient hill-and-pond style and the more recent stroll-garden style, in which various landscape features are gradually revealed along winding paths. The garden features artificial hills contoured around a pond, a waterfall, and an island while carefully placed rocks also play a leading role. Among the major architectural elements of the garden are wooden bridges, stone lanterns, a viewing pavilion, the Torii or gateway, and a Shinto shrine.

The Jacques Marchais Museum of Tibetan Art on Staten Island was established in 1945 to foster an interest in Tibetan and Himalayan art. The museum sits atop Lighthouse Hill, one of the highest points on the Eastern Seaboard. The museum is designed to resemble a small Himalayan mountain monastery.

Wave Hill is a twenty-eight-acre public garden and cultural center in the Bronx overlooking the Hudson River and Palisades. Its mission is to celebrate the artistry and legacy of its gardens and landscapes, to preserve its magnificent views, and to explore human connections to the natural world through programs in horticulture, education, and the arts. It's a great place to walk, think, and appreciate the beauty in a world that often seems ugly.

Strawberry Fields in Central Park is a living memorial to the world-famous singer, songwriter, and peace activist—John Lennon. During his career with the Beatles and in his solo work, Lennon's music gave hope and inspiration to people around the world. His campaign for peace lives on, symbolized at Strawberry Fields. Visiting this peaceful place inspires one to "give peace a chance."

Bear Mountain State Park is situated in rugged mountains rising from the west bank of the Hudson River. The park features the Perkins Memorial Tower. It's atop the mountain and, if you climb it, affords spectacular and breathtaking views of the park, the Hudson Highlands, and Harriman State Park.

St. Paul's Chapel at Columbia University is a rich mixture of Italian Renaissance, Byzantine, and Gothic styles. The chapel contains an Altar for Peace by George Nakashima, a wooden table with natural edges in his signature style. St. Paul's is referred to as "Columbia's most spectacular building" in the *Eyewitness Guide to New York* and is a New York City Landmark. It is open daily for prayer and meditation. I prefer its small size, sense of repose, and quiet beauty to the more spectacular and energized Cathedral of St. John the Divine and Riverside Church, both of which are nearby and worth pilgrimages in their own right.

Green-Wood Cemetery in Brooklyn is 478 magnificent acres of hills, valleys, glacial ponds, and paths, throughout which exists one of the largest outdoor collections of nineteenth and twentieth century statuaries and mausoleums. Four seasons of beauty from century-and-a-half-old trees offer a peaceful oasis to visitors, as well as to its 560,000 permanent residents, including Leonard Bernstein, Boss Tweed, Charles Ebbets, Jean-Michel Basquiat, Louis Comfort Tiffany, Horace Greeley, Civil War generals, baseball legends, politicians, artists, entertainers, and inventors.

The Ramble in Central Park is composed of thirty-eight acres of winding pathways between 73rd and 78th Streets. Described by Frederick Law Olmsted as a "wild garden," the Ramble's maze of woodland trails contrasts spectacularly with the formality of nearby attractions, such as the Bethesda Terrace. The Ramble is often noted for its bird watching opportunities, where bird watchers can catch a glimpse of some of the approximately 230 species found in the woods. I like to sit on a bench and look at the Gill, the man-made stream that runs through the Ramble, where I have seen movements in the underbrush that I am certain were made by raccoons or some kind of unexpected creature. The Ramble always seems a place to connect and make new friends.

Prospect Park in Brooklyn has a century-and-a-half tradition of horseback riding with a 3.5-mile bridle path through scenic and varied terrain. The bridle path begins at the Park Circle entrance and continues alongside the Lake to the Long Meadow and the Midwood. If you can ride and want to lose the sense of being trapped in the city, take a pilgrimage to nature on the back of one of God's noblest creatures, because nothing is more uplifting than an early-morning canter around the park.

Pilgrimages Around the World

Machu Picchu in Peru stands 2,430 meters (close to 8,000 feet) above sea-level, in the middle of a tropical mountain forest, in an extraordinarily beautiful setting. It was probably the most amazing urban creation of the Inca Empire at its height; its giant walls, terraces, and ramps seem as if they had been cut naturally in the continuous rock escarpments. The natural setting, on the eastern slopes of the Andes, encompasses the upper Amazon basin with its rich diversity of flora and fauna.

The Isle of Iona is a tiny Scottish island, of typically Hebridean beauty, that holds a unique place in the history of Scotland and kindles the imagination of thousands who journey there each year. Iona is considered one of the holiest places in the world. Some of this is due to the pioneering Christianization efforts of the early Irish missionary, St. Columba. But the island's fame was long that of a place where the veil was thin and the "otherworld" could be reached even by the humblest of pilgrims.

Assisi is a small Umbrian town in Perugia, Italy, best known as the birthplace of St. Francis of Assisi— patron saint of Italy, founder of the Franciscan order, and one of the most popular saints in history. Assisi's main attraction is the thirteenth century Basilica di San Francesco, which contains the sacred relics of Francis and beautiful frescoes of his life. And there are at least seven other churches well worth visiting for their history, beauty, and connection with Francis or his friend, Clare. The town of Assisi, with its Roman ruins, winding medieval streets, and sacred shrines, has been a major pilgrimage destination for centuries and is today one of the most popular tourist destinations in Italy. I personally have a dream of one day leading a twelve-step retreat in one of Assisi's many monasteries.

Antarctica Andrew Denton once said that if Antarctica were music it would be Mozart; if art, Michelangelo; if literature, then Shakespeare. Yet ultimately it is something much greater than all of those—namely, the only place on Earth that is still as it should be. He hoped we would never tame it.

Mysterious and vast, Antarctica—the "white continent" at the bottom of the world—is like no other place on Earth. A land of glittering ice, majestic peaks, and dazzling beauty, it has been a haven for millions of years for migratory birds, whales, seals, and other marine mammals. On a trip in 2011, I found myself awestruck and speechless for five days as we floated through the most otherworldly landscape I've ever experienced. Afterward, we sailed to Patagonia, yet another place worth a pilgrimage.

Agrigento in Sicily used to be the ancient Greek city Akragas. The city has preserved a large sacred area with seven monumental Doric temples. Though earthquakes, wars, and stone quarries have upset most of the original constructions, the Valle dei Templi comprises some of the largest and best-preserved ancient Greek buildings outside of Greece, along with many other Greek and Roman sites. It's here that I feel connected to the glory that was Greece and the grandeur that was Rome.

Mt. Croagh Patrick in County Mayo, Ireland, is visited each year by a million pilgrims and tourists who make the trek to the top of this holy mountain to pray, do penance, or just enjoy the majestic views. Before the arrival of Christianity, the Celtic people regarded the mountain as the dwelling place of the deity Crom Dubh. The pilgrimage to the top of the sacred mountain is an act of penance. Accordingly, some undertake the journey barefoot or even on their knees. With shoes, it's an easy ascent and you'll have lots of company.

Yoshino and Omine, Kumano Sanzan, and Koyasan are sites in Japan set in the dense forests of the Kii Mountains overlooking the Pacific Ocean. They are rooted in both the ancient tradition of nature worship in Japan and in Buddhism. The sites and their surrounding forest landscape reflect a persistent and extraordinarily well-documented tradition of sacred mountains over the last 1,200 years. The area, with its abundance of streams, rivers, and waterfalls, is still part of the living culture of Japan and is much visited for ritual purposes and hiking, with up to fifteen million visitors annually. Each of the three sites contains shrines, some of which were founded as early as the ninth century.

Christmas in Bethlehem, the city where Jesus was born, is a major event. Some of Bethlehem's Christmas celebrations would be familiar to Europeans and North Americans—the streets are strung with Christmas lights, there is a Christmas market, and Christmas plays are performed. But other events, which are the most important religiously, are special to Bethlehem and in keeping with the traditions of the Holy Land. These consist of multiple services and processions led by many different Christian denominations, including Catholic, Anglican, Greek Orthodox, Ethiopian, Armenian, and more.

The Mnajdra Temples are three conjoined Neolithic temples on the southern coast of Malta. Mnajdra occupies a spectacular and isolated position on a rugged stretch of coast overlooking the Mediterranean Sea and the isle of Fifla. To me, the temples represent the eternal human longing to discover the divine and to connect with it. The setting offers a sense of the magnificence of creation, while the temples evince a yearning to know and to find something that is greater than ourselves.

The Bodhi Tree ("Tree of Awakening," also known as the **Bo Tree**) in Bodhgaya, India, is a direct descendant of the tree under which Siddhartha Gautama attained enlightenment. After forty-nine days of meditation, it was here that Siddhartha Guatama became the Buddha, the "Enlightened One." According to Buddhist tradition, Siddhartha Gautama finally abandoned years of rigorous fasting and asceticism by accepting milk and honey from a young woman. He then sat down beneath the Bodhi Tree and vowed not to move until he attained enlightenment. Today, the Bodhi Tree is a favorite place for pilgrims to meditate and contemplate.

CHAPTER NINE

Labyrinths

In the previous chapter we discussed traveling the world on pilgrimage. This chapter offers an alternative. Ever since the medieval period, people who could not go on expensive pilgrimages have walked a labyrinth instead. The idea behind the labyrinth was that it could represent a spiritual journey through one's mind and heart and could be used as an act of devotion, allowing the "pilgrim" or walker to pray, meditate, and connect with the divine while inside its confines. In such a way, the spiritual benefits of a genuine pilgrimage could be accrued without having to leave home.

"What's a labyrinth?" you might ask. Let me be philosophical, and first define a labyrinth in terms of what it is not. A labyrinth is not a maze. The two terms are not synonymous, although they are related and often confused with one another. A maze is a network of paths and hedges designed as a puzzle through which one has to find a way, both to get to the center and to get back out. The primary purpose of a maze is to get lost. A secondary purpose is to encourage people to stroll and converse.

I have been attracted to mazes since I was a boy when I saw the Laurel and Hardy film, *A Chump at Oxford* on television. In the film the two comedians are enrolled at Oxford University and are the victims of a series of pranks from a group of nasty, snobbish undergraduates. They are sent off into a maze in order to get a pass to see the dean and quickly become lost. One of the students dresses as a ghost in order to frighten Stan and Ollie, and while they sit on a bench to sleep, the ghost's hand comes through the hedge to help Stan smoke his pipe and cigar (substituting for Stan's actual hand). The scene is both hilarious and scary. I've never forgotten it.

Two famous mazes I've enjoyed are the Hedge Maze in Williamsburg, Virginia, and the Hampton Court Maze outside of London. Since mazes are usually lined with tall hedges or thick shrubbery, I once embarrassed myself by gossiping about a friend who unfortunately was in the maze as well and on the other side of a hedge. If nothing else, the experience taught me to be careful of what I say, even if I think I'm not being overheard. Or maybe just to be kinder about people.

In contrast to a maze, there are no puzzles or tricks at all to a labyrinth. The way to the center and back is clearly defined. Unlike mazes, which are only seen outside, a labyrinth can be constructed indoors as well as outdoors. There are no hedges to obscure your way in a labyrinth; it's usually laid out on a flat stone, marble, turf, gravel, or canvas surface with painted lines, rocks, or short shrubbery to mark the boundaries. I once walked a labyrinth that was constructed after a snowstorm at the General Theological Seminary in Manhattan—of course it was only temporary, using the transitory material at hand.

The purpose of a labyrinth is entirely different from that of a maze. The maze is a social tool. The labyrinth is a spiritual tool. Being in a maze reminds me of my active addiction when I was lost, confused, and frustrated. A labyrinth reminds me of recovery where I can see my way clearly, know the way out, and am centered. Both have become metaphors for different aspects and periods of my life.

Both labyrinths and mazes have a long history and originally they were all called labyrinths. There is evidence, for instance, of labyrinths in drawings from the Neolithic and Bronze periods. What their religious or cultural significance may have been is unknown. The famous labyrinth at Knossos in Crete, where sacrifices were made to the fabled Minotaur, was actually a maze. Besides the Cretans, the Egyptians and Etruscans built indoor labyrinths, largely for decorative purposes. There are examples of labyrinths in ancient India, Ireland, and in cave drawings in New Mexico. The Romans constructed labyrinths as protective and decorative symbols on the mosaic floors of civic buildings and villas. They were also constructed outdoors as a playground for children and as a test of skill for soldiers on horseback. The desire to represent the vagaries of life through a labyrinth seems to have been almost universal.

During the medieval period, labyrinths developed more complex forms and uses, reflecting the intricacies of faith, life, and philosophy in the medieval ethos. They began to be constructed in churches and cathedrals, rather than civic buildings and palaces. These labyrinths were elaborately laid out in colored marble and tiles on the floors of church naves. Probably the most famous of these is at Chartres Cathedral, where the labyrinth constructed in the early thirteenth century survives to this day and has become an object of pilgrimage for modern visitors. Many other examples survive as well, such as the beautiful one in St. Quentin, France. I have personally walked the very fine labyrinth in the chapter-house of Bayeux Cathedral, also in France. It measures twelve feet across and is composed of circles of tiles ornamented with shields, griffins, and fleur-de-lis, separated by bands of small, plain black tiles.

Labyrinths and mazes were known in literature up to the Renaissance, although the terms were used interchangeably. In the retelling of the legend of Theseus and the Minotaur in *A Midsummer Night's Dream*, Shakespeare has Titania say in Act II:

"The nine-men's-morris is fill'd up with mud,

And the quaint mazes in the wanton green

For lack of tread are undistinguishable."

She is referring to the English custom of building turf labyrinths on village greens for the purpose of ritual dances.

After the late medieval period, mazes and labyrinths separated in meaning and the terms settled into how they are used today. Mazes for social and decorative purposes continued to be built in the gardens of royal palaces and of wealthy landowners. Labyrinths as spiritual symbols fell into disuse and disrepair. Many were destroyed, like the one in Rheims Cathedral, France, where an officious priest objected to children playing in it and had it removed in the late eighteenth century.

It wasn't until our own time that labyrinths went through a revival. In the early 1990s, a priest from Grace Episcopal Cathedral in San Francisco, Canon Lauren Artress, led a group of pilgrims to Chartres where they removed the pews covering the Chartres labyrinth and walked it as a meditation exercise. When she returned home, Canon Artress prevailed upon Grace Cathedral to build two labyrinths, one indoors and one outdoors. Since then she has formed an organization, Veriditas, whose mission is to connect people to the labyrinth. Walking the labyrinth is a spiritual practice that quiets the mind, opens the heart, and grounds the body. Their vision is that the labyrinth experience nurtures the invisible web of connections between individual destiny and service to others, the global community, and the planet.

Lauren Artress hit a nerve when she reintroduced labyrinths in a spiritual, not specifically religious, form to the United States. Labyrinths are currently being used worldwide as a way to quiet the mind and recover a balance in life. They are used to encourage meditation, insight, self-reflection, stress reduction, and to discover innovation and celebration. They are open to all people as a nondenominational, cross-cultural blueprint for well-being. The practice of labyrinth walking integrates the body with the mind and the mind with the spirit. They can be found in medical centers, parks, churches, schools, prisons, memorial parks, spas, cathedrals, and retreat centers as well as in people's backyards.[18]

I am a vigorous proponent of labyrinth walking. I first walked the indoor labyrinth at Grace Cathedral in 1998. Later, in 2008, I took the facilitator training at Grace. I've written poetry about my experiences in the labyrinth to express the spiritual benefits to myself and to my recovery from addiction. Wherever I live, I find a labyrinth and try to walk it once a month. I have introduced friends, parishioners, and program people to the labyrinth. I've walked labyrinths by myself, with a close friend, with a small group, and with a hundred people under the full moon. I always come out in a spiritually better state than when I entered.

So, what does the labyrinth actually do spiritually? For me, it's a way to feed my spiritual hunger, the feeling all addicts have that there is more to life than what we are experiencing. Even in recovery there is always the risk that I can become bored with life and feel drained. There will be times when my imagination is not igniting and few symbols carry meaning for me. Walking the labyrinth is a profoundly effective practice to get out of this kind of spiritual funk and to nourish my soul. It brings me refreshment, calm, and sometimes even answers to vexing problems—or at least a direction in which to go.

I have learned, for instance, that praying with my body as well as my mind—that is, walking slowly and deliberately over a preordained path—is enormously helpful. I also use music when I'm in the labyrinth. The labyrinth forces me to engage my whole self in prayer by using my body, mind, and spirit stimulated by the movement and music. This is much different from kneeling in church or sitting at home.

Different things happen to different people when they walk the labyrinth. I follow two rules: follow the path and don't be distracted. When I enter I follow a routine that allows me to first calm myself in the presence of God, to connect with the people and causes that are dear to me, to attain a consciousness of a world greater than me and beyond me, to converse with God, and to possibly find guidance for problems I find vexing or nagging.

Labyrinths, by the way, come in different sizes. Some have five circles, others seven or nine, and the largest have eleven circles (like Chartres and Grace Cathedral). The protocols inside the labyrinth are simple and easy to follow. There's no time limit when you're in the labyrinth, but I usually spend between twenty and forty minutes when I'm in one. Nor do you have to walk it alone. The labyrinth is an experience that can be shared with others without disturbing your own inner reflections. Just step off the path for a moment if someone else is passing. Silence is the rule, so refrain from commentary and use headphones if music is part of the experience for you.

How you walk the labyrinth and what happens inside is highly personal. When I walk a labyrinth I follow a routine. First, I stand at the beginning of the path, breathe deeply, and clear my mind. When I start walking I repeat a short prayer. Sometimes I use the Serenity Prayer, sometimes the Third Step Prayer from my twelve-step fellowship, and sometimes the Jesus Prayer. I keep saying the prayer until my mind is filled with nothing but the prayer. At that point I feel relaxed and calm. Then I begin to pray for people by name. I pray for my family, my students, and my parishioners. I pray for people in recovery. I pray for my brother and sister members of the Order of Urban Missioners. I pray for people whose stories I've read in the news. I pray for people who don't like me and people at whom I am angry.

I keep praying for others until I reach the center. At the center, I pause and I pray for myself. I consider any decisions I have to make. I identify problems I am facing. I ask God for guidance and direction. I carry my problems with me on the journey out of the labyrinth. I try to hear the small, still voice of my Higher Power. I do my best to listen for answers and for the will of God. As I near the end of the walk I express my gratitude for the good things in my life and the successes I have had. I thank God for God's love and for the love of others. I pray that I will love more.

Walking the labyrinth has been compared to a dance or a waltz. The waltz might be seeking, discovering, communicating. It might be naming a sorrow, healing, desiring to connect with others. Whatever your dance is, the labyrinth can help you find what you are looking for.

Traversing the labyrinth is like taking a tour through the curves and folds of your own brain. Finding yourself at the center, you realize that you were everywhere on the path, as well. Wherever you go, there you are. And yet, there is a momentous poise of being there at the center.

For people who practice a program of meditation, prayer, and self-reflection, the labyrinth can be a precious tool, especially if passionately pursued. For me, it has been a path of grace.

Three Prayerful Questions Times Two

REV. JOHN T. FARRELL

What have I done for my recovery?

What am I doing for my recovery?

What should I be doing for my recovery?

What have I done for another addict's recovery?

What am I doing for another addict's recovery?

What should I be doing for another addict's recovery?

From *Guide Me in My Recovery: Prayers for Times of Joy and Times of Trial* by The Reverend John T. Farrell, PhD. © 2010 Central Recovery Press.

CHAPTER TEN

Retreats

Have you ever been so stressed and overwhelmed that you just wanted to get away from modern life and all its perils? To a place of serenity and peace? To a place with no television, wireless Internet, cell phones, or other technological distractions? To a place where silence is valued and where people speak in modulated tones; a place where you can pray, meditate, and just relax? To a place where the only people you meet are seeking similar respite or whose presence is dedicated to helping you? To a place where the permanent residents are willing to listen to you with sympathy and insight—a place from which you'll come home refreshed and renewed?

Well, there is such a place—many in fact. And they offer just the kind of rest and refuge you are looking for. They are called "retreats."

A retreat is a temporary withdrawal from the world where people can leave their everyday cares and refresh themselves in an environment conducive to contemplation, transformation, and renewal. The purpose of a retreat is to energize our bodies, minds, and spirits by granting us time to find serenity. Retreat-goers act on the belief that it is crucial to escape from the bombardment of sounds, images, demands, and obligations in their lives and to take time for their minds and hearts to come to stillness. In that way, they can hear the small, still voice inside that is God.

Retreats aren't for everyone, but many people in recovery find them useful. People go on retreat for a number of reasons that generally focus on positive personal change and practice, such as to

- Rediscover themselves and their purpose in life.
- Pray and meditate deeply.
- Relax and be rejuvenated.
- Reflect, ponder, listen, and gain clarity.
- Reestablish meaning in their lives.
- Find healing and comfort.
- Renew their faith.
- Seek answers to perplexing problems.
- Enjoy silence.
- Mourn or grieve a loss.
- Make a crucial decision.
- Write a Fourth Step.
- Do a Fifth Step.

Like many of the spiritual practices described in this book, retreats are not an especially new or novel approach to spiritual growth. As the Romans liked to say, *nihil novi sub sole*—that is, "There is actually very little under the sun that is new" when it comes to spiritual practice. Instead there are methods and ideas we reinvent and rework for our own purposes and fit into our own times and situations.

Dr. Gerald G. May, one of the best authorities on addiction, suggests that addicts who pursue spiritual growth in recovery may need to set aside their penchant for newness and novelty in their spiritual lives.[19] He explains how we are conditioned—both neurologically by our brains and culturally by modern society—to think that spiritual growth involves the discovery and collecting of new data and new insights. We assume that we have to "accumulate" something to show for our growth, and we thereby inadvertently increase our attachments. In reality, spiritual development and maturation require the exact opposite. It cannot be collected and packaged, but is rather a process of transformation, where we unlearn and let go of old ways and habits. The act of transcending and liberating and cleansing cannot happen on command or by instruction. Rather than taking control and "doing" it, we have to "let it happen" through divine grace.

There is no better way to cleanse, liberate, and redeem our thoughts and spiritual aspiration than by taking a retreat, and getting away from our busy, hectic, stressful lives and just taking a rest and breathe a little more freely.

Once you decide to go on a retreat, other decisions will have to be made as well. Where does one actually go on a retreat? What happens when you get there? There are a variety of retreat centers where one can go away for a day, for a weekend, a week, or even longer. Some are religious, some are not. All of them welcome pilgrims and seekers. You should pick one that suits your needs and your personality. In what follows I will describe various types of retreats and recommend some places where addicts in recovery will feel comfortable.

Types of Retreats

DIRECTED RETREATS

In a directed retreat the participants gather together to discuss a common theme. There will be a retreat master or facilitator who leads discussions and is often available for private meetings. If the retreat is held at a religious facility, you may be invited to participate in services, but usually these are optional. These retreats are often for both men and women, but, if you prefer, you can find retreats that are specific to men and women. There are also retreats for specific groups. Over the course of my life I've been on clergy retreats, faculty retreats (while at Fordham University), and gay retreats. I've also been a retreat master, which, while a grueling task, is a most rewarding labor of love.

Silent Retreats

In a silent retreat the participants observe a rule of silence either throughout the entire retreat or during specified times. There will be a retreat master who will give talks throughout the day, assign readings, and perhaps meet with you for a one-on-one consultation. In a silent retreat, the retreat master is often a trained spiritual director as well. Silent retreats are usually at monasteries and conventions. Jesuit retreats are often silent, while those run by Benedictines observe the Great Silence between 8:00 P.M. and 8:00 A.M.

Twelve-Step Retreats

Twelve-step retreats are exactly what the name implies. They focus on spiritual growth through the Twelve Steps in the context of a traditional retreat. This kind of retreat includes talks from retreat masters who are usually in recovery themselves, worship services designed for people in recovery, and opportunities for Fourth and Fifth Step work. When I conducted twelve-step retreats I offered an Episcopal healing service quite different from the Benny Hinn/Oral Roberts productions you see on television. It involved asking God for the healing power of acceptance and freedom from fear, the laying on of hands in blessing, and anointing with oil. For some people this can be a spiritually powerful experience and the high point of their retreat.

PRIVATE RETREATS

A private retreat offers the opportunity to simply get away from it all for a brief time with rest and spiritual recharging of one's personal goals. Many retreat centers let people check in for a day, a weekend, or for longer just to walk, read, rest, pray, seek counsel, and participate in worship. There are some helpful books for private retreats. For instance, Saint Anthony Messenger Press publishes a series of short books called *A Retreat with* . . . . Each book uses the writings of a particular spiritual master to lead you on a self-directed retreat. Another publishing house, Word Among Us Press, prints a similar series called *Companions for the Journey: Praying with* . . . . This series tends to be more ecumenical in outlook and includes some notable poets who wrote from a spiritual perspective. I would highly recommend *Praying with Julian of Norwich*, *Praying with Hildegard of Bingen*, *Praying with Dante*, and *Praying with Francis of Assisi*. And, if I ever get off my duff, maybe I will one day write *Praying with John Donne*.

WELLNESS RETREATS

These retreats are strictly secular and are often run for a profit. They offer certain kinds of spa treatments, massages, aromatherapy, holistic healing, healing remedies, and the like.

SELF-DIRECTED RETREATS

Years ago I lived in Maryland and worked in an extremely stressful job that was the catalyst for a long bout of clinical depression. I occasionally felt close to burn-out. One of my spiritual remedies was to take the day off, pack a lunch, and drive to Bon Secours, a retreat center outside Baltimore run by an order of nuns. In the morning, I would sit in their Japanese garden, watch the carp in the pond, listen to music, read, and meditate. Then I'd enjoy my lunch and feed the fish. In the afternoon, I'd walk their beautiful labyrinth, take a nap in a lounge or in my car, and finally go listen to the sisters chant vespers in the chapel at 5:00 P.M. Then I'd drive home, a better man for having been on my mini-private retreat, and understanding why retreats are often called "spiritual vacations."

Some Recommendations

For your spiritual vacation, I would like to make some recommendations. These are representative only. There are numerous places to go on retreat throughout the world. There are retreats for everyone. I will try to list places that I've visited, want to visit, or have heard about. This should give you some idea of what's available. I apologize that many of them are on the Eastern seaboard, but I had a bias toward those I know, have actually visited, or where I know someone who has. You'll be able to find an appropriate place in your own area, I promise. Of course, there are many resources available that list retreat houses. One that I've found useful is the Retreat Finder at *retreatfinder.com*.

In the meantime, here are some venues you might consider.

Matt Talbot Retreat Movement
(matttalbotretreats.org)

Matt Talbot retreats are held all over the country in various locations and are offered to either men or women. These retreats are specifically designed for people in recovery from alcoholism and are focused on the Twelve Steps. They are named after an Irishman, Matthew Talbot (1856–1925), whom many people revere as the Patron Saint of Alcoholics. According to the movement's website, a retreat at Matt Talbot provides recovering alcoholics with an opportunity to seek a deeper spiritual experience and to enhance their sober way of life. All who attend their retreats are alcoholics in recovery, and attendees come from a wide variety of religious and cultural backgrounds, representing all ages, races, and walks of life.

Matt Talbot retreats are highly structured. If you go, you will be asked to listen to seven reflections over the weekend, attend a Roman Catholic mass, and participate in religious devotions like the Stations of the Cross and Adoration of the Blessed Sacrament. Matt Talbot himself was a native Dubliner who had destroyed his life through abuse of alcohol. In 1884 he took a temperance society pledge of complete abstinence and remained sober for the rest of his life. He did this by means of daily mass, spiritual reading, extreme ascetical practices, and helping other alcoholics.

Dan Egan Retreats

(atonementfriars.org/our_missions_and_ministries/retreats.html)

Dan Egan Retreats are similar to Matt Talbot Retreats and are designed for recovering addicts. They are held in various locations throughout the United States, most notably at Graymoor Monastery in Garrison, NY. Father Dan Egan was a Graymoor friar who was known as "The Junkie Priest," which is also the title of a book he wrote. Father Egan helped the addicts who established Narcotics Anonymous in New York City in the early 1980s and was a spiritual mentor to many in recovery. These retreats are named in his honor.

Villa Palazzola

(palazzola.it)

In many ways, after Ireland, Italy is my spiritual home. It was the center of early Christianity, the birthplace of monasticism, and it is rich with the history and beauty of a great culture immersed in devotion to God. So naturally, making retreats in Italy is something my soul longs for. Although there are many, many places in Italy to do this (one dream of mine is to lead a retreat for recovering addicts in Assisi), the Villa Palazzola is the place I recommend for first time retreatants. It's a spectacularly beautiful place built on the ruins of a Roman Consul's country estate near Castle Gandolfo, the Pope's summer residence above Lake Albano, eighteen miles south of Rome. It has been home to Carthusian, Cistercian, and Franciscan monks and friars and is now owned by the Venerable English College. On the grounds is a stunning thirteenth century church, Our Lady of the Snows, a medieval monastery, and classical Italian gardens. The Villa Palazolla offers accommodations for tourists, guided retreats, and personal retreats.

Karmê Chöling
Shambhala Meditation Center
(karmecholing.org)

Karmê Chöling is in Barnet, Vermont, and is a Buddhist retreat house that offers directed retreats and instruction in meditation in the Shambhala tradition. Its most unique feature is the availability of remote cabins for personal retreats. A silent, solo retreat there is known as a *lerung* and is part of the practice of Tibetan Buddhism.

The Esalen Institute
(esalen.org)

According to its mission statement, the Esalen Institute in California is "more than a retreat center or an educational institute. Anchored by the inspiring beauty of Big Sur and an unparalleled intellectual history, Esalen is a worldwide network of seekers who look beyond dogma to explore deeper spiritual possibilities; forge new understandings of self and society; and pioneer new paths for change." The progenitor of the human potential movement, Esalen offers retreats focused on yoga, meditation, discovering purpose and meaning, and releasing tension and trauma.

PENDLE HILL

(pendlehill.org)

Pendle Hill is a Quaker facility that welcomes all persons for spirit-led learning, retreat, and community and those who are seeking the divine within themselves. Its values are focused on Quaker principles of simplicity, education and dialogue, community, sustainability, silent worship, and social justice. Pendle Hill provides accommodations, spacious grounds, workshops, and retreats. A unique feature of Pendle Hill is its long-term residence program that offers participants opportunities to grow spiritually and learn to live in harmony and community.

LITTLE PORTION FRIARY

(littleportionfriary.net)

Little Portion Friary in Mount Sinai, NY, on Long Island is the home of a group of Franciscan friars who belong to the Episcopal Society of St. Francis. According to their website, the friars "support your journey by offering our home as a place for prayer, reflection, retreats, meetings of all kinds, weddings, spiritual growth, engagement, and rest. We hope that you'll find

Little Portion a place where you can be yourself. We're committed to supporting you in finding your way to a joyous spirituality." To this end, they run directed and personal retreats, offer spiritual direction, have one-day retreats called "quiet days," and sponsor a number of unique programs. My favorite is their monthly labyrinth walk where people gather in the evening on the night of a full moon for dinner in the friary, then go outside to walk their beautiful labyrinth under torch light, and end with a meditative service of prayer and music in the Taize style (characterized by simple, repetitive phrases set to a tuneful melody). The Little Portion friars also occasionally offer directed retreats to the gay and lesbian community. Upon departure, you can take a loaf of their delicious homemade bread with you.

Eastern Point Retreat House
(easternpoint.org)

If you've ever dreamed of a quiet, restful place by the sea, then Eastern Point is the place for you. Eastern Point is run by the Society of Jesus, the Jesuits, and specializes in retreats based on the "Spiritual Exercises" of St. Ignatius Loyola discussed in an earlier chapter. Working from the "Exercises" as their founder designed them, Eastern Point conducts the purest and most complete versions of the eight- and thirty-day directed retreats in the United States. These are not for the fainthearted but are ideal for the spiritually mature and are well worth the effort.

The magnificent setting, with its craggy rocks, waves, and tides, stirs the soul and enhances the sense that you are in a thin place at a thin time.

ISABELLA FREEDMAN JEWISH RETREAT CENTER
(isabellafreedman.org/jewish-retreats/elatchayyim)

Also known as the Elat Chayyim Center for Jewish Spirituality, the Isabella Freedman Jewish Retreat Center is located in Falls Village, CT. According to its website, it offers "transformational and cutting-edge retreat experiences . . . that draw on the wisdom of Jewish tradition and reflect the values and consciousness of our evolving society. Experiential approaches to Jewish learning, ritual, and prayer are designed to help us all on our search to cultivate awareness of the divine presence in all aspects of life." To this end, retreatants practice contemplative silence and prayer. Integral to the experience is the creation of *mishpacha* (family) groups. These groups serve as safe emotional spaces where participants can express the insights, struggles, challenges, and surprises that they may be experiencing as the retreat progresses. Another unique feature is a children's program.

HOLY CROSS MONASTERY
(holycrossmonastery.com)

The Holy Cross Monastery in West Park, NY, is the place I know best. I have been attending retreats there for almost thirty-five years. It is a Benedictine community of Episcopal monks who are noted for their hospitality, erudition, wit, and love of gourmet food. Over the decades, I have gone there on personal retreats, directed retreats, clergy retreats, and twelve-step retreats. The Order of Urban Missioners has its annual retreat there. In 2012, I went to Holy Cross to experience the *Triduum*, the three days of Christ's passion, death, and resurrection. They even have a labyrinth overlooking the Hudson River that I have walked many times. Their list of retreat programs is impressive (see their website). Holy Cross is my favorite place, and I recommend it highly.

On a final personal note: It is a serendipitous irony that I wrote this chapter while on an annual clergy retreat for the Diocese of New York. It was a directed retreat and 140 priests listened to our new bishop, Andrew Dietsche, talk about our spiritual lives and how we might follow a rule of holy living as part of our priestly vows. Besides the retreat portion, there was plenty of time for shared fellowship, recreation, conversation, worship, and prayer. The most wonderful thing about the retreat was its venue: a dude ranch in Ulster County, New York. The Rocking Horse Ranch *(rockinghorseranch. com)* may sound like a strange place for a bunch of priests to recharge themselves spiritually, but the ranch works for us as we annually turn it into a sacred place of refreshment, a kind of portable thin place.

"Ride a horse and find God!" That's my motto at Rocking Horse Ranch.

CHAPTER ELEVEN

Mindfulness and Mirth

In his famous assessment of the metaphysical poets, especially
John Donne, Dr. Samuel Johnson complained that "The most
heterogeneous ideas are yoked by violence together; nature and art are
ransacked for illustrations, comparisons, and allusions; their learning
instructs, and their subtlety surprises; but the reader commonly
thinks his improvement dearly bought and, though he sometimes
admires, is seldom pleased."[20] My own readers may think I'm doing
the same thing by writing a chapter that yokes together the concepts
of mindfulness and mirth. What does one have to do with the other?

Mindfulness is a not a new term. It has its roots in Old English
myndful meaning "of good memory." Later on, it came to mean
"the trait of staying aware or being attentive." In psychology, it refers
to being in touch with our feelings and being aware of the present
moment. In this context, to be mindful means to be nonevaluative
and nonjudgmental. The modern concept of mindfulness derives

from Eastern spiritual and religious traditions like Zen Buddhism. Today, psychologists recognize that mindfulness can provide assistance for people suffering from anxiety, depression, and addiction. For recovering addicts, working the steps may be regarded as a method to attain greater mindfulness or awareness of the world outside and around us, rather than the inward-looking, self-destructive self-absorption that delineates active addiction.

Mirth, too, is an old term, coming from the Old English *myrgð*, meaning "joy and pleasure." Its current meanings include "gladness, amusement, and gaiety, especially when expressed by laughter." One of my favorite words is *mirthquake*, which refers to "entertainment that excites convulsive laughter." It was coined in 1928 in reference to Harold Lloyd movies.

So how do mindfulness and mirth come together, aside from being a great alliteration? We know that as recovering addicts we need to be mindful—that is, aware of who we are, what we must do to heal ourselves, and to learn empathy and compassion. We also know that laughter, especially the ability to laugh at ourselves, is a way of knowing ourselves, is a source of healing, and a means of expressing empathy and compassion toward others. Healthy laughter is evidence of joy in recovery, serenity in our hearts, and love of others. To these ends, mindfulness and mirth can become natural companions on our journey toward wholeness.

The more we know about treatment for addiction, the more we understand that laughter is an effective form of healing. Humor can be used in treatments for stress, anxiety, depression, even pain—so why not for addiction? After all, the disease of addiction includes all those components and then some. In fact, for many, mirth is the elixir of life.

Self-described "laughologist" Albert Nerenberg, who produced a documentary on the topic called *Laughology: The Movie*, has said this about laughter: "I believe that laughter is itself a language, and the primary positive form of communication between people. It is a powerful way to reach people who might otherwise be unreachable. Because laughter is naturally contagious, it can be used to affect people who would otherwise be withdrawn. Laughter causes powerful destressing and calming changes in people and can elevate mood."[21]

Mindfulness, too, acts as an excellent antidote to the emotional and spiritual ravages of addiction. In modern psychology, mindfulness comprises three components: *remembering*, *awareness*, and *attention*. I believe that the Twelve Steps will also lead addicts down the path of mindfulness, although not necessarily in quite the tidy order that therapists and gurus would wish for us. The Fourth, Fifth, Eighth, Ninth, and Tenth Steps are certainly about *remembering* (that is, remembering to be aware). The First, Second, Third, Sixth, Seventh, and Eleventh teach us *awareness* (that is, relating compassionately to life). And Step Twelve is all about *attention* (that is, focused awareness). For those who are interested in pursuing the concept of mindfulness in its Buddhist form, there is a form of mindful meditation I will discuss more fully in the next chapter.

There is an old Yiddish proverb that says, "What soap is to the body, laughter is to the soul." Soap makes us clean, which is also a colloquialism for complete abstinence from all drugs, so the analogy is doubly apt. But humor and laughter are only healthy for us in recovery if they are motivated by the compassion, awareness, and nonjudgmentalism engendered by mindfulness.

Mohandas Gandhi once remarked, "If I had no sense of humor, I would long ago have committed suicide." We all know people, even in recovery, who lack humor or practice a cruel kind of wit. These tend to be people we wish to avoid. They themselves are often unhappy and struggling. We want to say to them, "Lighten up! Recovery should be about joy and mirth, not grimness and perpetual drama." When I associate with program people, I don't want to feel like I'm living in the real-life version of *Mean Girls.*

I have always had a sense of humor, so I've never understood people who don't. But my humor hasn't always been benign. When I was in my active addiction I used my gift to make people laugh for shabby ends. I could be mocking and derisive. I could and would laugh at others' expense. I was a master at exposing the supposed flaws, failures, and foibles of others. I did this because of my own unhappiness. I was miserable and unconsciously wanted others to suffer as well. My destructive humor grew out of my own self-hatred and insecurity and feelings of not being loved. Ironically, the people I ridiculed the most were the people I valued and admired. I simply had this relentless, addictive need to tear down what I couldn't have for myself. In recovery, this has changed. My humor is far more gentle and often used to relive tensions. It is also self-referential— that is, I can laugh at my own follies. In fact, the ability to laugh at myself is one of the benchmarks of the self-esteem and self-love I've acquired in recovery.

I have often wondered why some people don't have a sense of humor. Some people seem to be so serious and sad all the time. It actually disconcerts me to say something funny and have them not react. Or, even worse, when they take my jokes literally and say, "I don't think that's very funny." For me, these are people who are not fun to be around. I especially struggle when I have to work with someone like that. I have to work very hard at accepting them for who they are and where they are at.

We all know how to laugh. No one has to teach us that. But can we develop a sense of humor? I think so. Here are some hints:

- Consider what it is you find funny. Mirthquakes like *The Simpsons*? Satire like *South Park*? Stand-up comedy? Cartoons? Dirty jokes? The poetry of Alexander Pope? Be aware of what tickles your funny bone. Cultivate this area so it spills over into other areas.

- Remember that having a sense of humor is not about being funny or making jokes. It's the capacity to see the lighter side of life.

- Before you dismiss something as not funny, remember the context and motivation. There is a classic *Mary Tyler Moore Show* called "Chuckles Bites the Dust" where the characters cope with the death of a colleague who has died in a bizarre accident—a professional clown, he had dressed as the character Peter Peanut, and a rogue elephant at a circus parade tried to "shell" him, causing fatal injuries—by laughing and making jokes. Prim Mary is disgusted and chastises them for their irreverence. However, at Chuckles' funeral, when everyone else is appropriately somber, Mary starts to laugh uncontrollably. The pastor leading the service encourages her to "let it all out," but Mary is so embarrassed, she begins to cry hysterically.

- Be objective. People are always going to laugh when you slip on a banana peel or drop a tray in the cafeteria.

- Try to understand why others are laughing at something. You may end up finding it funny too. Watch, listen, and learn. You have a sense of humor. We all do. Find your inner clown.

So, as we grow more mindful and self-aware of who we are in recovery, we can, should, and possibly must develop the ability to see the funny and ironic side of life. Developing a healthy sense of humor is really the test of our ability to grow spiritually, which is why I believe mindfulness and mirth to be crucial spiritual practices. The next time something unpleasant or unexpected happens, don't wait to whine at a meeting, don't call your sponsor, don't fall apart, and don't let it spoil your day. Instead, take a deep breath and try to find the lighter side of things. It's there. I promise you. You may have to look hard for it. But when you do find it, you'll smile. You may even laugh. And then you can go about your business of living life on life's terms.

An Arrow Prayer for Times of Duress

REV. JOHN T. FARRELL

Breathing in: I love . . .

Breathing out: even my shadows.

Breathing in: I love . . .

Breathing out: even my enemies.

From *Guide Me in My Recovery: Prayers for Times of Joy and Times of Trial* by The Reverend John T. Farrell, PhD. © 2010 Central Recovery Press.

CHAPTER TWELVE

Breathing and Yoga

I am neither an authority on Eastern religions in general nor Hinduism and Buddhism in particular. But I know many of us in the West, in and out of recovery, have found solace and growth in the spirituality associated with Hinduism, Zen, Buddhism, and other Eastern religions. I believe there is much that people in recovery can learn from these ancient traditions. Thomas Merton, one of my spiritual icons, was fascinated with Buddhist monasticism and meditation and spent the last part of his life studying the correlations between them and their Western counterparts. In fact, Roman Catholic monk Wayne Teasdale wrote this of him: "Thomas Merton was perhaps the greatest popularizer of interspirituality. He opened the door for Christians to explore other traditions, notably Taoism . . . Hinduism and Buddhism."[22] To me, Merton's open-mindedness has been a beacon in my recovery.

We have already learned how the Buddhist concept of mindfulness has been adapted by modern psychology. You also saw how I took this concept and coupled it with mirth and the development of self-awareness through the steps leading to a healthy sense of humor. In this chapter, I'd like to discuss two Hindu and Buddhist spiritual practices that fellow recovering addicts have assured me have been a source of inspiration for them in their recoveries. The first is the practice of breathing as the keystone to mindful meditation, and the second is yoga. Considering them as part of your spiritual life speaks to the flexibility and the ability to learn from a myriad of sources that is crucial to a healthy spiritual recovery.

Mindful breathing has a long pedigree in the Hindu tradition, dating back to the great scholar, Buddhaghosa, who lived during the fifth-century in India and Sri Lanka. The form of breathing taught by Buddhaghosa was designed to calm and focus the practioner's mind. To that end, mindful breathing is referred to as a *samatha*, or calming practice, which is different from a *vipassana*, or insight practice. This distinction is why I didn't include breathing in the chapter on meditation, which focused more on insight into the nature of reality and our connection to the divine. Mindful breathing is also known as *anapanasati*, a term that means "breathing in and out." In this form of practice, the breath is used as the object of our attention to which we return every time we notice that the mind has wandered.

The goal of mindful breathing is bringing about a sense of serenity, peace, and calm. There are many methods of breathing meditation, but here's how I have adapted it for use in my own daily regimen of prayer and meditation:

- To begin, I play some soothing music.
- Then, I sit in a comfortable chair keeping my spine straight.
- I close my eyes and begin to breathe (not that I haven't been breathing already, of course, but now I do so consciously and mindfully).
- I focus on my breathing only and nothing else. I imagine there's a balloon in my stomach and that the balloon inflates when I breathe in and deflates when I breathe out. I notice the sensations in my abdomen as the balloon inflates and deflates.
- I focus on my stomach as it gently rises and falls.
- When thoughts come to mind or sounds intrude, I notice them and gently push them away so I can return to my breathing.
- I continue to let the imaginary balloon go, inflate and deflate, up and down.
- People who just breathe mindfully say ten minutes is a proper amount of time to derive the benefits of its relaxing properties.

In my case, however, I'll deviate from this norm since I use mindful breathing as a preparation for insight meditation. I practice *lectio divina* before my breathing, selecting a word from my reading—Love, Justice, Peace, Forgiveness, etc.—as a mantra. I'll then repeat my mantra in unison with my breathing. After five minutes or so, I'll begin to prayerfully meditate on the theme of my mantra and see where it leads me.

Some practioners recommend breath counting as a means of keeping the mind focused on breathing, letting all other thoughts drift away. For this method, Nicole Dante recommends that you sit up straight in a relaxed, meditative position, taking some easy, deep breaths, and closing your eyes. With each exhale, start counting from one to ten. Once you get to the number ten, begin again at one. Sometimes you may find yourself counting higher then ten, in which case you just bring your awareness back to your breath, and begin another cycle at one.[23]

Breathing and yoga are closely related. According to the *Westminster Dictionary of Christian Spirituality*, "Yoga is one of the six main philosophical schools of Hinduism . . . [and] came to emphasize liberation or isolation."[24] As a school it is concerned with concentration, attainment, physical power, and liberation. In more common usage, "yoga" has come to denote a type of physical, mental, and spiritual discipline originating in India and utilized in both Hinduism and Buddhism. In the United States and the Western world, yoga is used chiefly to describe a type of exercise that provides both health and spiritual benefits. As a form of meditation it is often conflated with Zen, a form of Buddhism.

Yoga is not universally admired in the West. The Roman Catholic Church has expressed reservations and has claimed that yoga "can degenerate into a cult of the body" and "could also lead to psychic disturbance and, at times, to moral deviations."[25] Fundamentalist and evangelical leaders have made similar statements, although not as elegantly as the Vatican.

I disagree with the above disapproval, preferring to listen to the experience of thousands of recovering addicts who practice yoga and say it enhances their recoveries. These people see yoga as a safe nonaerobic form of exercise that relaxes them, improves their health, and brings them closer to serenity. Many see it as a form of meditation as well. I cannot and will not argue with them.

Yoga comes in a variety of different forms, including:

- *Hatha*, which is sometimes called "beginners' yoga." If you practice *hatha*, you will start with a stretching class coupled with simple breathing exercises and seated meditation.
- "Hot" or *Bikram* yoga, which synthesizes traditional yoga methods practiced in a heated enviornment

and consists of sessions that last exactly ninety minutes.

- *Kundalini* (breathing) yoga, which is designed to expand practioners' sensory awareness and intuition.
- *Ashtanga* yoga, which teaches how to match one's breath with the movement of yoga postures. Doing so will help generate internal heat, purifying the blood, and leading to a light and strong body as well as a calm and concentrated mind.

Based on research and listening, I can make the following points about yoga.

It encourages integration. The primary goal and effect of yoga seems to be integration. It is not just meditation, but a "moving" meditation, which combines the benefits of "sitting still mindfulness" with the fruits of physical exercise. A friend has told me that the most enjoyable aspect of yoga for her personally is moving with the breath. Yoga coordinates breathing with movement (the instructor will literally say, "on the next inhale do this . . . on the next exhale do that"), which is a powerful way of aligning oneself with one's body and of coming into the present moment.

It provides an holistic workout. As a physical exercise, yoga has the advantage of being a full body workout, involving all the muscles of the body in almost every pose, treating it as an integrated whole. Also, yoga stimulates, massages, and conditions not just the outer layers of the body but also the internal organs. Many of the twisting and stretching movements actually stimulate glands and gently massage organs like the liver, the kidneys, and the intestines, thereby helping to flush out toxins and optimizing function. To me, the most attractive feature here is the connection aspect. Connection is one of the deepest spiritual principles, and to live spiritually is to connect with God—or one's Higher Power, Source of Being, Inner Being, Higher Self, God Self, or Spirit.

It leads to flexibility and release. One of the underlying ideas in yoga is that the spine is representative of the self: the more flexible our spine, the more flexible, adaptable, and resilient we will be in our lives. Physical rigidity and stiffness, especially in the neck, shoulders, back, and lower back, can mirror mental and emotional or spiritual rigidity. By repeated gentle stretching, combined with breath that allows us to move deeper into each pose, we become increasingly flexible; and the more flexible we are in yoga, the more flexible we become in life.

I have heard from friends who do yoga that they often experience profound emotional releases from holding certain poses and stretching out certain muscles and tissues. One friend in particular told me she would feel waves of sadness or sudden bouts of extreme irritation from stretching certain parts of her body. This is based on the idea of "cell memories" getting released—unlocking the chemicals of substances we ingested during active addiction, as well as chemical states of distress we recorded in our cells during traumatic experiences. For recovering addicts, letting go and releasing past toxicity—be it physical, emotional, or spiritual—is hugely beneficial. Yoga can be a powerful way of addressing and releasing the emotional pain and physical damage that has crystallized in our bodies. In this way, yoga is a perfect complement to the steps for many people in recovery.

It is non-doctrinaire. While yoga has its roots in Hinduism and dates back many thousands of years, as an activity it is free of any religious doctrine. This makes it appealing to many who seek a deeper spirituality but are wary of religious orthodoxy. The vast majority of yoga classes do not include explicit guided meditation or any trappings of religion beyond the basic gentle Zen and Buddhist ethos that animates the practice. In reality, yoga is taught primarily as a physical exercise in the West, with a friendly, welcoming, and accepting atmosphere. Often the closing greeting, "Namaste" (translating roughly as "the divine light in me recognizes and acknowledges the divine light in you") is the only indication that something "spiritual" is going on. Perhaps at the beginning of the class the instructor may encourage people to "set an intention" for the class and to "let go" of the day and everything prior to that present moment, but one would be hard-pressed to find "doctrine" in such an appeal.

People with a strong Western attitude toward religious faith need not worry that doing yoga presents any kind of conflict with their beliefs.

It is universally accessible. Yoga can be practiced by anyone regardless of age, fitness level, or flexibility. There are no entry requirements and there is no pressure or push to achieve, like there can be in a typical workout or "spin class." Most yoga classes I've learned about include experienced yogis and first-timers stretching side by side, and everyone gets something from the class because the poses are designed to put one right up to one's own current limit, wherever that may be, and not beyond.

I would like to conclude this chapter by folding my hands in a praying gesture, bowing to you, and saying "Namaste." As mentioned above, this is the traditional closure of a yoga session in which the teacher and the students bow to each other, acknowledging their mutual divinity. I would like to expand on that a bit and say, "The teacher in me bows to the teacher in you." This should remind us all that we are simultaneously teachers as well as students in recovery.

A Prayer of Connection

REV. JOHN T. FARRELL

Source of Being, most of my life is focused on myself and the people I know, the places I visit, and the things I encounter. But, even in my most mundane encounters and moments, if I listen carefully or if I pause for just a second, I can hear your small, still voice and sense your presence around and within me. Help me recognize those moments of connection amidst the "busy-ness" and distractions of my life. Let me cherish and be nourished by your loving presence in my life, in the lives of those whom I meet, and in the life of the world around me. Amen.

From *Guide Me in My Recovery: Prayers for Times of Joy and Times of Trial* by The Reverend John T. Farrell, PhD. © 2010 Central Recovery Press.

CHAPTER THIRTEEN

Some Things to Avoid

While I encourage folks to seek out the God of their own understanding in any and all ways they feel inspired to, I also want to offer some words of caution. Sometimes, especially early in recovery, we can get carried away with a certain focus or activity, and here, as in all things, I urge the reader to seek out balance and to enjoy the process of spiritual and personal growth at the pace and incremental stages of natural unfolding.

There are the obvious things to avoid: Dubious cults and pseudospiritual movements that engage in any form of physical, sexual, or mental abuse, fraud, greed, or forceful brainwashing. The problem, however, is that subversive and harmful organizations rarely advertise themselves as such, so what follows below is a list of characteristics and warning signs I would encourage you to look out for. Be vigilant with any group or organization that

- Is deceptive in their recruitment, not forthright about who they are or who they are affiliated with. This is in counterpoise to twelve-step organizations' policy of attraction not promotion, and our accessibility to all through our literature and open meetings.

- Consciously attracts the vulnerable, the needy, and those in crisis for the purposes of exploitation rather than to help them as laid out in twelve-step programs.

- Creates a sense of obligation and guilt, as opposed to gratitude.

- Demands fealty to a charismatic leader whose readings or sayings dominate the organization, rather than practice the principle of anonymous and selfless service.

- Offers answers to and for all areas of life instead of letting you find your own as part of a new way of life.

- Demands total immersion in their way of living and thinking, neither brooking opposition nor encouraging independent thinking.

- Isolates members from family and friends, coerce behaviors, and control access to information, especially information that is critical of the organization.

- Is excessively secretive and casts a spell on its members with hints at the existence of esoteric knowledge that only they possess.
- Views outsiders as enemies, rather than encouraging members to become productive and functioning members of society, as do twelve-step organizations.
- Seeks to attract new members through glamour, celebrity and famous existing members.
- Promises a spiritual short-cut for the fickle and uncommitted.
- Provides facile, ahistorical, and potentially dangerous answers about addiction, especially those that actually encourage the use of drugs.
- Promotes the idea that gays can be "converted" from homosexuality by a study of the movement's principles. This theory flies in the face of recovery principles that allow gays (and any kind of minority) to accept their identities and be who they are.
- Denigrates women and relegates them to subservient roles. In contrast, twelve-step groups honor all members as equals.
- Promotes the use of an outmoded spiritual practice known as mortification—the practice of inflicting pain on oneself or depriving oneself of necessities for reasons of spiritual gain and punishment of one's transgressions.

The life of active addiction is filled with pain. Who needs more? During my addiction I punished myself enough for several lifetimes. Recovery is hard, yes, but its promises are joy and serenity, not more pain and mortification. I find my answers now through the Twelve Steps, meetings, sponsorship, service, helping others, and growing spiritually. I don't want easy answers. I don't want quick fixes. I don't want others to do my thinking for me. With God at my side, I shall recover.

CHAPTER FOURTEEN

Recommended Reading

INTRODUCTION

English Spirituality: An Outline of Ascetical Theology according to the English Pastoral Tradition by Martin Thornton (Wipf & Stock Publishers, 2012).

The New Westminster Dictionary of Christian Spirituality edited by Phillip Sheldrake (Westminster John Knox, 2013).

A NOTE ON TERMINOLOGY

The God Instinct: Heeding Your Heart's Unrest by Tom Stella (Sorin Books, 2001)

What Do We Mean When We Say God? by Deidre Sullivan (Doubleday, 1991).

PRAYER

Guide Me in My Recovery: Prayers for Times of Joy and Times of Trial by John Farrell (Central Recovery Press, 2010).

Pray All Ways: A Book for Daily Worship Using All Your Senses by Edward Hays (Forest of Peace, 2007).

Sacred Space: The Prayer Book 2013 by the Irish Jesuits (Ave Maria Press, 2012).

MEDITATION

Christian Meditation: Your Daily Practice by Laurence Freeman (Novalis, 2007).

Quiet Mind: A Beginner's Guide to Meditation edited by Susan Piver (Shambhala, 2008).

The Soul Workout: Getting and Staying Spiritually Fit by Helen H. Moore (Central Recovery Press, 2010).

JOURNALING

Simply Soul Stirring: Writing as a Meditative Practice by Francis Dorff (Paulist Press, 1998).

At a Journal Workshop: Writing to Access the Power of the Unconscious and Evoke Creative Ability by Ira Progoff (Tarcher, 1992).

MENTORING

The Mentee's Guide: Making Mentoring Work for You by Lois J. Zachary and Lory A. Fischler (Jossey-Bass, 2007).

Soul Friend: Spiritual Direction in the Modern World by Kenneth Leech (Morehouse, 2001).

WRITING A RULE OF LIFE

Everyday Simplicity: A Practical Guide to Spiritual Growth by Robert J. Wicks (Sorin Books, 2000).

The Rule of Benedict: A Spirituality for the 21st Century by Joan Chittister (Crossroad, 2010).

Benedict's Way: An Ancient Monk's Insights for a Balanced Life by Daniel Homan and Lonni Collins Pratt (Loyola Press, 2005).

LECTIO DIVINA

The Dance of Life: Weaving Sorrows and Blessings into One Joyful Step by Henri Nouwen (Ave Maria Press, 2005).

John Donne: The Major Works by John Donne (Oxford, 1990).

Opening to God: Lectio Divina and Life as Prayer by David G. Benner (IVP Books, 2010).

Of Character: Building Assets in Recovery by Denise D. Crosson (Central Recovery Press, 2009)

RITUAL

Creating Rituals: A New Way of Healing for Everyday Life by Jim Clarke (Paulist Press, 2011).

Return to the Sacred: Ancient Pathways to Spiritual Awakening by Jonathan H. Ellerby (Hay House, 2010).

PILGRIMAGE

The Art of Pilgrimage: The Seeker's Guide to Making Travel Sacred by Phil Cousineau (Conari Press, 2012).

The Spirit in the Desert: Pilgrimages to Sacred Sites in the Owens Valley by Brad Karelius (BookSurge, 2009).

Open Spaces Sacred Places: Stories of How Nature Heals and Unifies by Tom Stoner and Carolyn Rapp (TKF Foundation, 2008).

LABYRINTHS

Walking a Sacred Path: Rediscovering the Labyrinth as a Spiritual Practice by Lauren Artress (Riverhead, 1996).

Labyrinth: Illuminating the Inner Path by Brian Draper (Lion UK, 2011).

MINDFULNESS AND MIRTH

Between Heaven and Mirth: Why Joy, Humor, and Laughter Are at the Heart of the Spiritual Life by James Martin (HarperOne, 2011).

Not Quite Nirvana: A Skeptic's Journey to Mindfulness by Rachel Neumann (Parallax Press 2012).

RETREATS

Wilderness Time: A Guide for Spiritual Retreat by Emilie Griffin (HarperOne, 1997).

Retreat: Time Apart for Silence and Solitude by Roger Housden (Harper Collins, 1995).

Monastery Guest Houses of North America: A Visitor's Guide by Robert J. Regalbuto (Countrymen Press, 2010).

BREATHING AND YOGA

Christian Yoga: A Daily Christian Meditation Guide For Your Practice by Julie Schoen (Little Pearl, 2012).

The Tao of Natural Breathing: For Health, Well-Being, and Inner Growth by Dennis Lewis (Rodmell Press, 2006).

Yoga and the Twelve-Step Path by Kyczy Hawk (Central Recovery Press, 2012).

Some Things to Avoid

Encyclopedic Dictionary of Cults, Sects, and World Religions: Revised and Updated Edition by Larry A. Nichols, George A. Mather, and Alvin J. Schmidt (Zondervan, 2006).

In the Beauty of the Lilies by John Updike (Alfred A. Knopf, 1996).

RECOMMENDED
READING

Daily Inventory

REV. JOHN T. FARRELL

Am I making sufficient efforts to develop my concept of a Higher Power?

How well have I sought to improve my conscious contact with God?

Did I pray and meditate today?

When I was wrong, did I promptly admit it?

Was I in contact with another recovering addict today?

Was I unkind or cruel to others, sarcastic or caustic?

Did I nurture resentments?

Was I generous and patient with others?

Did I respect people around me, especially those in authority and those over whom I have authority?

Did I gossip maliciously and detract from another's character?

Was I judgmental?

Did I express my displeasure by being slow, sullen, and passive aggressive?

Did I exercise self-control or was I angry and impatient?

Was I truthful and honest?

Was I a good friend?

Was I a good sponsor?

Was I grateful?

Was I a good example of recovery?

Will I do better tomorrow? How?

From *Guide Me in My Recovery: Prayers for Times of Joy and Times of Trial* by The Reverend John T. Farrell, PhD. © 2010 Central Recovery Press.

NOTES

1 David R. Leigh, "Thin Places," *Rethinking Faith* (blog), 2006, http://www.rethinkingfaith.com/post/2925550027/poem-thin-places.

2 St. Athanasius, *De Incarnatione Verbi Dei*, 54.3.

3 *Book of Common Prayer* (New York: Church Publishing Company, 1979), 856.

4 1 Chronicles 29: 11–12.

5 Excerpt from the traditional Jewish prayer *Al Chet* (recitation of sins).

6 Mark Batterson, *The Circle Maker: Praying Circles Around Your Biggest Dreams and Greatest Fears* (Grand Rapids, MI: Zondervan, 2011), 43.

7 First mentioned by Thomas of Celano in *Vita Beati Francisci* ("*The Life of Blessed Francis*," often called the "*First Life*"), in 1228.

8 Father Michael Duffy, "'The Happiest Man on Earth,' the Eulogy for Father Mychal Judge," delivered at the Funeral, September 15, 2001, at St. Francis of Assisi Church, New York City. Published in Cyrus M. Copeland, ed., *A Wonderful Life: 50 Eulogies to Lift the Spirit* (Chapel Hill, NC: Algonquin Books of Chapel Hill, 2006), 221–230.

9 Michael Ford, *Father Mychal Judge: An Authentic American Hero* (Mahwah, NJ: Paulist Press, 2002), 104.

10 Ibid., 28.

11 Ibid., 124.

12 "The Last Homily of Father Mychal Judge," FDNY Engine 73, Ladder 42, Bronx, NY, September 10, 2001. Available at www.mychalsmessage.org.

13 Eileen Egan, *Dorothy Day and the Permanent Revolution* (Erie, PA: Benet Press, 1983), 19.

14 Ibid., 25.

15 Adele Ahlberg Calhoun, *Spiritual Disciplines Handbook: Practices that Transform Us* (Downers Grove, IL: InterVarsity Press, 2005), 35–39.

16 Ibid.

17 See http://www.randomactsofkindness.org/kindness-ideas.

18 Veriditas and the Labyrinth Society jointly maintain a world-wide labyrinth locator at http://labyrinthlocator.com/home.

19 Gerald S. May, *Addiction and Grace: Love and Spirituality in the Healing of Addictions* (New York: HarperOne, 2007), 105–6.

20 Samuel Johnson, *Lives of the Most Eminent English Poets: With Critical Observations on their Works* (London: Frederick Warne & Co., 1870), 9.

21 Albert Nerenberg, as quoted by Alison Palkhivala in "Could Addiction be a Laughing Matter?" on Sobriety Home's website at http://www.sobriety.ca/laughter-therapy-article.htm.

22 Wayne Teasdale, *Mystic Heart: Discovering a Universal Spirituality in the World's Religions* (Novato, CA: New World Library, 1999), 39.

23 Nicole Dante, "Mindful Breathing Exercise," *LiveStrong.com*, May 26, 2011, http://www.livestrong.com/article/332439-mindful-breathing-exercise/.

24 Gordon S. Wakefield, ed., *Westminster Dictionary of Christian Spirituality* (Philadelphia, PA: The Westminster Press, 1983), 398.

25 Cardinal J. Ratzinger, "Letter to the Bishops of the Catholic Church on Some Aspects of Christian Meditation" (Rome, Italy, from the offices of the Congregation for the Doctrine of the Faith, October 15, 1989, the Feast of Saint Teresa of Jesus), 28–29.